Steck-Vaughn

Vocabulary Connections

www.HarcourtAchieve.com
1.800.531.5015

ILLUSTRATIONS

Cover: Ed Lindlof
Content Area Logos: Skip Sorvino

Marty Blake 5, 29, 53, 77, 101; Nancy Carpenter 55–57, 59, 84–87, 89; Heidi Chang 36–39, 41, 49, 52, 103–105, 107; Eldon Doty 12–15, 17, 125; Robert Frank 7–9, 11, 96–97, 100; David Griffin 30, 78; Linda Knox 60–63, 65; Mike Krone 32–33, 44, 46, 71–74, 76, 116, 118; Ann Neumann 23–26, 28, 91–92, 94, 125; Marti Shohet 79–81, 83, 120–122; Samantha Smith 19–20, 22, 125.

PHOTOGRAPHY

p. 5 © Tom Brakefield/Bruce Coleman; p. 6 © Tom McHugh/Photo Researchers, Inc.; p. 18 © James R. Holland/Black Star; p. 29 © Michael K. Keller/CORBIS; p. 30 © Lawrence Migdale/Getty Images; pp. 42, 43 © Yoram Kahana/Shooting Star; p. 47 © Culver Pictures, Inc.; p. 54 © New York Public Library Picture Collection, photo: Robert Rubic; p. 66 © MPTV.net; p. 67 © Hulton/Getty Images; p. 68 © Gene Lester/Hulton/Getty Images; p. 70 © Bettman/CORBIS; p. 77 © Mickey Gibson/Animals Animals; p. 90 © Ron Church/Photo Researchers, Inc.; p. 101 © Michael Keller/CORBIS; p. 102 © Henry Diltz/CORBIS; pp. 114–115 © Theo Westenberger/Gamma-Liaison; p. 119 © Paolo Koch/Photo Researchers, Inc.; p. 124 © Kenneth Murray/Photo Researchers, Inc.

ACKNOWLEDGMENTS

HarperCollins Publishers: Adaptation from *The Philharmonic Gets Dressed* by Karla Kuskin, illustrated by Marc Simont. TEXT COPYRIGHT © 1982 BY KARLA KUSKIN; ILLUSTRATIONS COPYRIGHT © 1982 by Marc Simont. Used by permission of HarperCollins Publishers.

J. Kellock & Associates, Ltd.: "Rhinos for Lunch and Elephants for Supper!" a Maasai tale retold by Tololwa Marti Mollel. Reprinted from Cricket magazine, July 1988. Copyright © 1988 by Tololwa Marti Mollel. Reprinted by permission of J. Kellock & Associates Ltd. on behalf of the author.

Little, Brown and Company: "How Spider Got a Thin Waist" from *The Adventures of Spider* by Joyce Cooper Arkhurst. Copyright © 1964 by Joyce Cooper Arkhurst. By permission of Little, Brown and Company.

Macmillan Publishing Company: Pronunciation Key, reprinted with permission of the publisher from the *Macmillan School Dictionary 2.* Copyright © 1990 Macmillan Publishing Company, a division of Macmillan, Inc.

Copyright © 1969 by Molly Cone from the book THE RINGLING BROTHERS published by Thomas Y. Crowell Company, Inc. Reprinted by permission of McIntosh and Otis, Inc.

Nancy Alpert Mower: From "Storm at Sea" by Nancy Alpert Mower. Reprinted from *Cricket* magazine, April 1987. Copyright © 1988 by Nancy Alpert Mower.

ISBN 1-4190-1989-9

8 9 10 11 12 1421 14 13 12 11
4500335087

TABLE OF CONTENTS

CONTENT AREA SYMBOLS

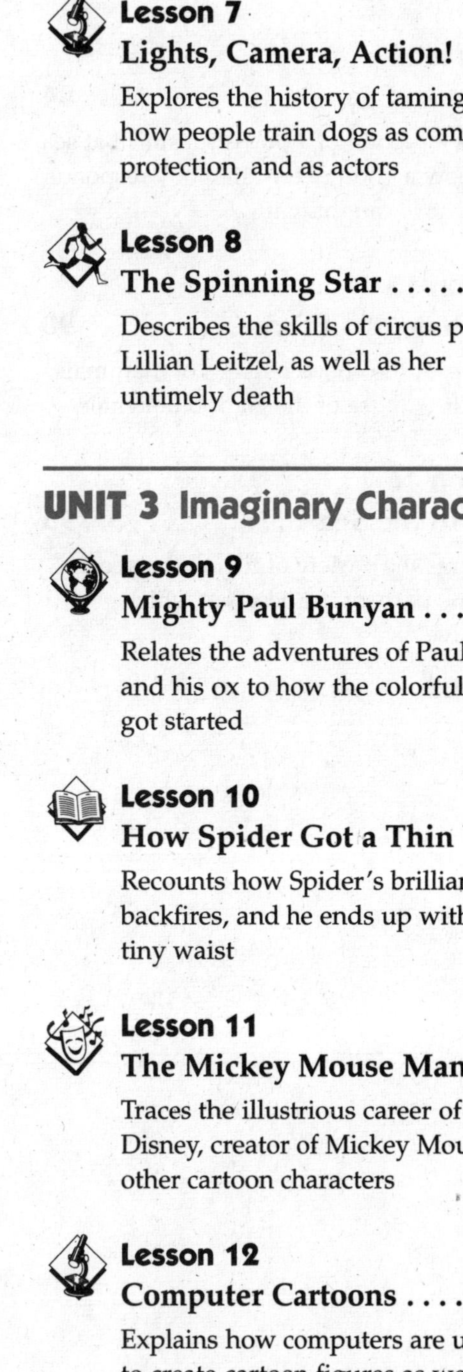

Literature · Social Studies · Science · Mathematics · Health · Fine Arts

JUNGLES AND TROPICS

The jungle is alive with sights and sounds. It is home to animals great and small. A thick, green blanket of plant life covers it. Rivers wind through it like snakes.

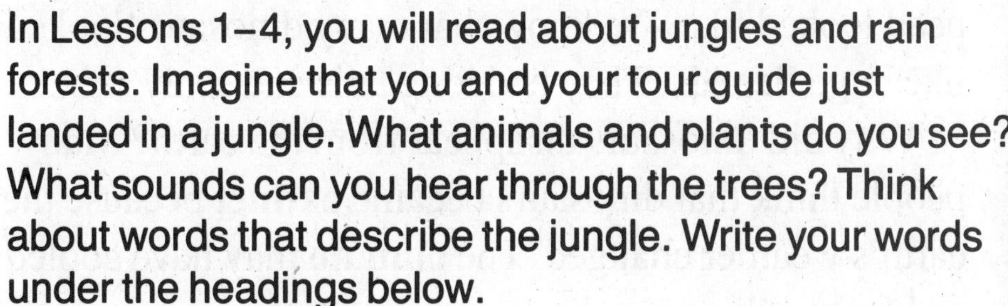

In Lessons 1–4, you will read about jungles and rain forests. Imagine that you and your tour guide just landed in a jungle. What animals and plants do you see? What sounds can you hear through the trees? Think about words that describe the jungle. Write your words under the headings below.

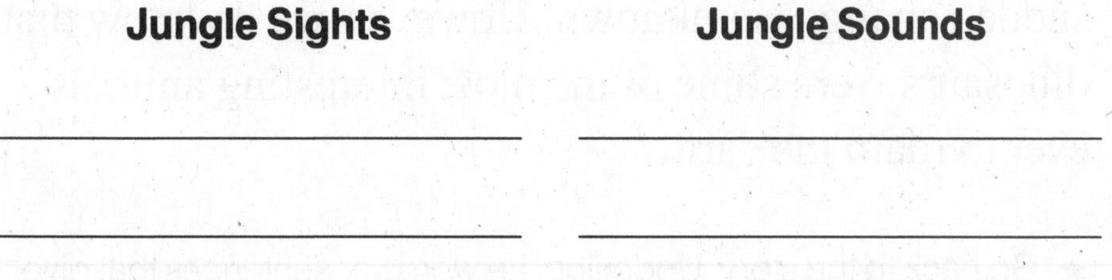

Jungle Sights	**Jungle Sounds**
______________________	______________________
______________________	______________________
______________________	______________________

★ Read the story below. Think about the meanings of the **boldfaced** words. ★

The Age of the Dinosaur

Imagine the earth 220 million years ago. Much of the land had warm weather all year. Rain fell often in some places, so they were **moist**. The heat and wet air caused thick bushes, twisting vines, and tall trees to grow. In this **jungle** and across the open plains, some remarkable animals began to appear.

Dinosaurs were a group of four-legged animals that ruled the earth for about 140 million years. Some dinosaurs were as tall as a three-story building. Others were as small as cats.

No one has ever seen a dinosaur alive. Dinosaur footprints, bones, and teeth were **preserved**, or saved, in the ground. These **fossils** are often found in rocks. The rocks were once the mud in which dinosaurs walked.

Studying fossils gives us facts about dinosaurs. The shape of a dinosaur's teeth gives us **information** about whether it ate meat or plants. Its **skull** tells us what its head looked like. We know that many dinosaurs looked like huge **lizards**. They had long tails and scaly skin.

Why did dinosaurs disappear from the earth? Many people think that dinosaurs became **extinct** because the earth's weather changed. The **climate** may have cooled suddenly, killing the dinosaurs. The cause of this sudden change is unknown. However, we do know that dinosaurs were some of the most interesting animals ever to roam the earth.

★ Go back to the story. Underline the words or sentences that give you a clue to the meaning of each **boldfaced** word. ★

CONTEXT CLUES

Read each sentence. Look for clues to help you complete each sentence with a word from the box. Write the word on the line.

moist	**dinosaurs**	**lizard**	**extinct**
skull	**preserved**	**jungle**	**climate**
fossils	**information**		

1. Many ________________ were powerful beasts.
2. There are books that have ________________ about what dinosaurs looked like and how they lived.
3. Dinosaur bones were ________________ in mud that hardened into rocks.
4. We know from studying ________________ that some dinosaurs had wings and could fly.
5. A ________________ shows head size and shape.
6. The long tail of some dinosaurs was like the tail of a ________________.
7. The dinosaurs walked in soft, ________________ mud.
8. Some dinosaurs ate plants in the ________________.
9. The ________________, or weather, was hot.
10. When the earth's weather turned cold, the dinosaurs may have died and become ________________.

Antonyms

Antonyms are words that have opposite meanings. Match the words in the box with their antonyms listed below. Write each word on the line.

extinct	moist	preserved	jungle

1. ruined ______________________
2. dry ______________________
3. living ______________________
4. desert ______________________

Dictionary Skills

A dictionary can help you find out how to say a word. Turn to page 133 in the Dictionary. Use the **pronunciation key** to help you learn how to say the vocabulary words in ( ) in the sentences below. Write the regular spelling for each word in ( ).

i it	**u** up	ə = **a** in ago
ī ice	**o** hot	

1. The (skul) is made of bone. ______________________
2. The (liz′ərd) climbed a tree. ______________________
3. We can learn from (fos′əlz). ______________________
4. The (klī′mit) got colder. ______________________
5. No one ever saw a (dī′nə sôr′). ______________________

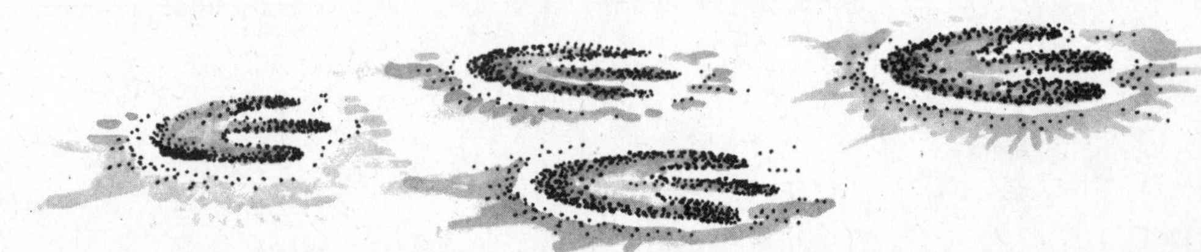

Hidden Message Puzzle

Write a word from the box next to each clue. To find the message, copy the numbered letters in the matching numbered boxes at the bottom of the page. Then you will know something that dinosaurs left behind.

dinosaur	skull	information	jungle
extinct	moist	preserved	climate

1. facts ☐☐☐☐☐☐☐☐☐☐☐ (box 3 = 1)
2. animal that lived long ago ☐☐☐☐☐☐☐☐ (box 4 = 3, box 8 = 6)
3. the weather in an area ☐☐☐☐☐☐☐ (box 6 = 4)
4. bone around the brain ☐☐☐☐☐ (box 1 = 10)
5. hot place with thick plants ☐☐☐☐☐☐ (box 3 = 8)
6. damp ☐☐☐☐☐ (box 2 = 2)
7. saved ☐☐☐☐☐☐☐☐☐ (box 1 = 5)
8. no longer living on earth ☐☐☐☐☐☐☐ (box 4 = 7, box 7 = 9)

ANSWER: ☐☐☐☐☐☐☐☐☐☐

1 2 3 4 5 6 7 8 9 10

GET WISE TO TESTS

Directions: Read each sentence. Pick the word that best completes the sentence. Mark the answer space for that word.

Some tests have letters in the answer circles. Fill in the circle next to your answer.

1. Powerful beasts called _____ lived long ago.
Ⓐ break Ⓒ fat
Ⓑ dinosaurs Ⓓ lizard

2. Many books have _____ about dinosaurs.
Ⓕ dry Ⓗ information
Ⓖ large Ⓙ surprising

3. Dinosaur bones were _____ in the ground.
Ⓐ preserved Ⓒ price
Ⓑ after Ⓓ climate

4. The bones buried in rock and mud are called _____.
Ⓕ fun Ⓗ slowly
Ⓖ fossils Ⓙ liking

5. Dinosaurs liked the warm air and thick plants in the _____.
Ⓐ bump Ⓒ jungle
Ⓑ pretend Ⓓ them

6. The jungle air was _____, or damp.
Ⓕ mop Ⓗ moist
Ⓖ skull Ⓙ afraid

7. Some dinosaurs had a tail like a _____.
Ⓐ long Ⓒ both
Ⓑ try Ⓓ lizard

8. A dinosaur's _____ can show its head size.
Ⓕ skull Ⓗ still
Ⓖ so Ⓙ moist

9. The weather, or _____, of the earth changed.
Ⓐ hold Ⓒ fossils
Ⓑ lost Ⓓ climate

10. Dinosaurs died and became _____.
Ⓕ ocean Ⓗ extinct
Ⓖ most Ⓙ sweet

Writing

Some dinosaurs were quiet animals that ate plants. But others were mean and scary. Many even ate other dinosaurs. Look at the picture of the dinosar on this page. Its name was Tyrannosaurus rex. Do you think it was friendly or fierce?

Use the lines below to describe this dinosaur. Include how you think it moved, what it ate, and how it protected itself. Use some vocabulary words in your writing.

I think Tyrannosaurus rex was a ____________

____

____

____

____

____

____

____

____

____

____

____

____

____

Turn to "My Word List" on page 131. Write some words from the story or other words that you would like to know more about. Use a dictionary to find the meanings.

★ Read the children's story below. Think about the meanings of the **boldfaced** words. ★

Rhinos for Lunch and Elephants for Supper!

In this African tribal tale, jungle beasts are frightened by a sound they hear in a cave.

After a **pleasant** visit with her aunt and a cool walk among the trees, the little **hare** had reason to be cheerful as she **approached** the cave where her den was hidden. But just as she was going to enter, there was a sound in the cave.

"A monster, a monster!" boomed a voice. "I eat rhinos for lunch and elephants for supper! Come in if you dare!" The hare **trembled** with fear and took to her heels. Along the path she met the fox and told him about the monster.

"Come, I'll get him out for you!" said the fox. When they got to the cave, the fox bared his teeth and barked, "Come out, great bully of a monster, before I sink my teeth into your neck!"

Once again the **terrifying** voice rocked the earth and echoed through the jungle, sending the fox scampering away with the hare close behind.

The two ran until they met the **leopard**, who offered to help. They all returned to the hole, and the leopard stuck out his claws. "Come out, big brute of a monster, before I claw your eyes out!"

The monster's voice ripped through the air, "I eat rhinos for lunch and elephants for supper! Come in if you dare!"

The leopard drew in his claws and went leaping away, followed closely by the fox and the hare. They did not stop till they met the rhino. "Come, I'll deal with him," said the rhino. At the cave, he drummed his massive chest and **snarled** into the opening. But before he could speak, the voice came thundering out, "I'm a monster, a monster! I eat rhinos for lunch and elephants for supper! Come in if you dare!"

Greatly alarmed, the rhino **bounded** away, followed by the other animals. Along the way they met the elephant and told him of the monster. "Come, follow me!" bellowed the elephant. "A good **thrashing** with my trunk ought to bounce him out!" But his bellowing did no good, and once again all the animals went crashing away from the frightening voice in the cave.

As all the animals went trooping by, a little frog **cautiously** peered out of his hole. "What's the matter?" he politely inquired, stopping the animals dead in their tracks. After hearing of the monster, the frog was thoughtful for a moment. "I'll drive him away for you," said the little frog, all calmness and confidence.

At the cave, he cleared his throat and boomed in at the monster, "I'm the great eater, the great eater! I eat rhinos for breakfast, elephants for lunch, and monsters for supper! I'm coming! I'm coming!"

The animals stood silently and watched the entrance to the cave. Out came a tiny caterpillar who looked up at the huge animals with a big, slightly sheepish grin. Rubbing her ears, she said in a very tiny voice, "Dear me, what an echo there is in that cave!"

From Rhinos for Lunch and Elephants for Supper!, by Tololwa Marti Mollel

★ Go back to the story. Underline any words or sentences that give you clues to the meanings of the **boldfaced** words. ★

USING CONTEXT

Meanings for the vocabulary words are given below. Go back to the story and read each sentence that has a vocabulary word. If you still cannot tell the meaning, look for clues in the sentences that come before and after the one with the vocabulary word. Write each word in front of its meaning.

trembled	pleasant	hare	approached
leopard	cautiously	bounded	thrashing
snarled	terrifying		

1. ____________________: carefully
2. ____________________: an animal like a rabbit
3. ____________________: shook
4. ____________________: growled
5. ____________________: frightening
6. ____________________: leaped
7. ____________________: beating
8. ____________________: cheerful, nice
9. ____________________: came closer
10. ____________________: large catlike animal with spots

CHALLENGE YOURSELF

Name two animals that people might find terrifying.

____________________ ____________________

Dictionary Skills

Guide words are the two words at the top of each dictionary page. They show the first and last words on a page. All the words in between are in ABC order. Decide which words from the box would go on each page. Write the words in ABC order.

hare	leopard	approached	cautiously
bounded	thrashing	terrifying	pleasant

after / head	last / toe
________________	________________
________________	________________
________________	________________
________________	________________

Synonyms

Synonyms are words that have the same or almost the same meaning. Match the words in the box with their synonyms listed below. Write each word on the line.

snarled	cautiously	pleasant	trembled

carefully ________________________

cheerful ________________________

shook ________________________

growled ________________________

GET WISE TO TESTS

Directions: Read the phrase. Look for the word or words that have the same or almost the same meaning as the boldfaced word. Mark the answer space for your choice.

Some tests have letters in the answer circles. Fill in the circle next to your answer. Be sure to cover the letter, too.

1. **trembled** in fear
   Ⓐ sang Ⓑ walked Ⓒ danced Ⓓ shook

2. **pleasant** visit
   Ⓕ scared Ⓖ sad Ⓗ cheerful Ⓙ terrible

3. the little **hare**
   Ⓐ rabbit Ⓑ fox Ⓒ jungle Ⓓ frog

4. **approached** slowly
   Ⓕ climbed down Ⓖ went backward Ⓗ came closer Ⓙ moved away

5. claws of a **leopard**
   Ⓐ jumping animal Ⓑ catlike animal Ⓒ doglike animal Ⓓ snakelike animal

6. the rhino **snarled**
   Ⓕ barked Ⓖ growled Ⓗ ate Ⓙ played

7. they **bounded** away
   Ⓐ walked Ⓑ crawled Ⓒ looked Ⓓ leaped

8. a **terrifying** sound
   Ⓕ beautiful Ⓖ sweet Ⓗ frightening Ⓙ happy

9. a good **thrashing**
   Ⓐ time Ⓑ meeting Ⓒ feeling Ⓓ beating

10. **cautiously** peered out
    Ⓕ happily Ⓖ carefully Ⓗ suddenly Ⓙ quickly

Writing

The jungle animals felt happy when the little caterpillar came out of the cave. Suppose the tale ended differently. Instead of a caterpillar, a monster like the one in the picture came out of the cave. What would the animals do? Would the monster be mean or friendly?

Write a new ending that answers these questions. Use some vocabulary words in your writing.

Turn to "My Word List" on page 131. **Write some words from the story or other words that you would like to know more about. Use a dictionary to find the meanings.**

★ Read the story below. Think about the meanings of the **boldfaced** words. ★

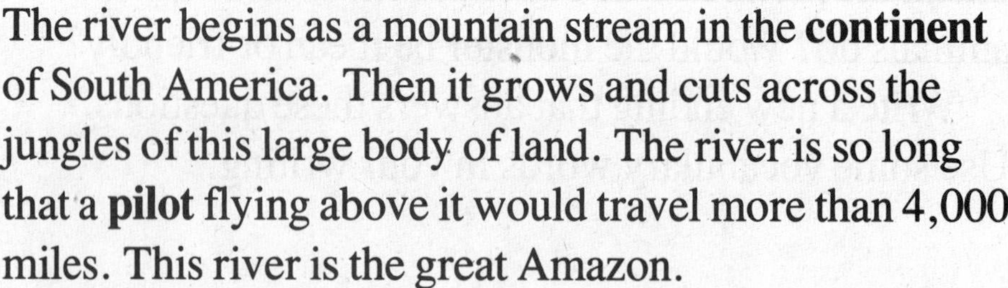

Amazon Riches

The river begins as a mountain stream in the **continent** of South America. Then it grows and cuts across the jungles of this large body of land. The river is so long that a **pilot** flying above it would travel more than 4,000 miles. This river is the great Amazon.

Early **explorers** risked their lives on the unknown waters of the Amazon. One explorer, Francisco de Orellana, searched nearby for a city of gold called El Dorado. De Orellana never found El Dorado, but he made other **discoveries.** Once he and his men met a group of fierce Indians who were women. De Orellana named them "Amazons" after women warriors in a Greek story. The river soon took the same name.

Today, the Amazon River area is still wild. It is full of life. **Alligators** with sharp teeth float like logs in the river. Insects such as **mosquitoes** whine and buzz in the air. Colorful birds, long snakes, and chattering monkeys all make their homes near the river.

At one time, trees along the Amazon provided **rubber**. The rubber was used to make tires and balls. Today, very little rubber comes from the Amazon. But **materials** to make many other things can be found there. Trees along the river are cut for **lumber**, and plants are used in medicines. There is mining for **minerals** like gold and iron. Sadly, millions of acres are being destroyed for ranches, roads, and resources. Amazon rain forests and jungles are in great danger.

★ Go back to the story. Underline the words or sentences that give you a clue to the meaning of each **boldfaced** word. ★

Using Context

Meanings for the vocabulary words are given below. Go back to the story and read each sentence that has a vocabulary word. If you still cannot tell the meaning, look for clues in the sentences that come before and after the one with the vocabulary word. Write each word in front of its meaning.

continent	**discoveries**	**rubber**	**pilot**
materials	**alligators**	**minerals**	**lumber**
explorers	**mosquitoes**		

1. ________________: wood used for building
2. ________________: people who search new places
3. ________________: what things are made of
4. ________________: a huge piece of land
5. ________________: things mined from the ground
6. ________________: natural material that bounces
7. ________________: flying insects that bite
8. ________________: new things found
9. ________________: a person who flies airplanes
10. ________________: big, dangerous animals living in rivers and swamps

Classifying

Each row groups words about the Amazon. Write each word from the box in the group where it belongs.

lumber	explorers	alligators
minerals	mosquitoes	

Amazon

Products: ______________ ______________

Animals: ______________ ______________

People: ______________

Cloze Paragraph

Use the words in the box to complete the paragraph. Reread the paragraph to be sure it makes sense.

pilot	discoveries	continent
minerals	material	

The largest country on the (1) ______________ of South America is Brazil. One of the most important (2) ______________ in Brazil took place near the Amazon. A helicopter (3) ______________ landed on dirt that had an orange (4) ______________ in it. He had found iron. Brazil became a source of iron, gold, and other (5) ______________.

GET WISE TO TESTS

Directions: Read each sentence carefully. Then choose the best answer to complete each sentence. Mark the space for the answer you have chosen.

Before you choose an answer, try reading the sentence with each answer choice. This will help you choose an answer that makes sense.

1. Minerals are mined in the _____.
Ⓐ ground Ⓒ trees
Ⓑ store Ⓓ sink

2. Alligators are dangerous water _____.
Ⓕ people Ⓗ minerals
Ⓖ animals Ⓙ vegetables

3. Explorers travel to new _____.
Ⓐ stores Ⓒ schools
Ⓑ lands Ⓓ backyards

4. Materials are used for _____ things.
Ⓕ dreaming Ⓗ wishing
Ⓖ saying Ⓙ making

5. A pilot flies a _____.
Ⓐ train Ⓒ bus
Ⓑ plane Ⓓ car

6. A continent is a huge piece of _____.
Ⓕ water Ⓗ trees
Ⓖ land Ⓙ roads

7. Discoveries are _____ things found.
Ⓐ wet Ⓒ new
Ⓑ terrible Ⓓ silly

8. A rubber ball will _____.
Ⓕ break Ⓗ bark
Ⓖ bounce Ⓙ sink

9. Lumber is _____ for building things.
Ⓐ rubber Ⓒ grass
Ⓑ wood Ⓓ rock

10. Mosquitoes can _____ you.
Ⓕ splash Ⓗ carry
Ⓖ swallow Ⓙ bite

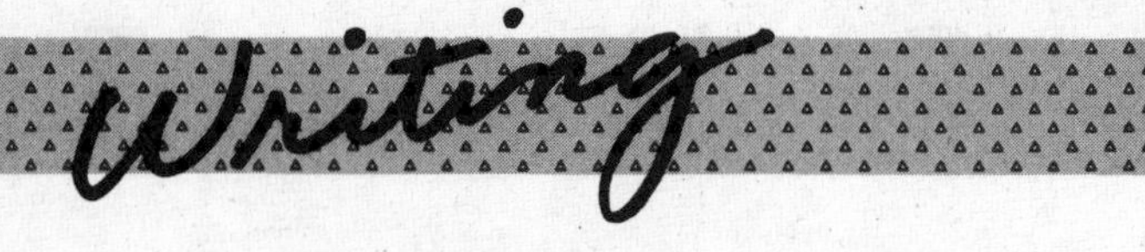

Explorers often write down the things that happen on their travels. Imagine that you are exploring the Amazon River.

Finish this page of a notebook you are keeping. Look at the picture to help you describe the things you saw and did today. Use some vocabulary words in your writing.

____
(Date)

Today was an exciting day on the Amazon. I came slowly around a bend in the river. Suddenly, ______

____

____

____

____

____

____

____

____

____

____

Turn to "My Word List" on page 131. **Write some words from the story or other words that you would like to know more about. Use a dictionary to find the meanings.**

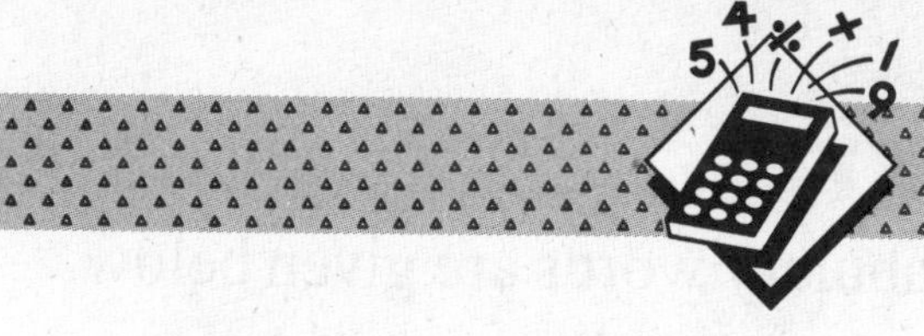

★ Read the story below. Think about the meanings of the **boldfaced** words. ★

A World Below the Trees

You are walking near the edge of a tropical rain forest. The jungle plants are so **thick,** so close together, that you must slowly push your way through. Then the jungle ends, and you enter the rain forest itself. Here the **distance,** or space, between the plants is greater.

A tropical rain forest is made up of different **levels.** The top level is a ceiling of treetops. Measured from the ground up, the treetops reach 100 to 200 feet in **height**. The middle level is made up of shorter trees and bushes. Here, many animals and insects live. The number of different kinds of insects alone is well over one **thousand**. Plants at the lowest level, the forest floor, are about a **meter** high, or just over 39 inches.

Jungles often grow at the edge of rain forests. But if you **compare** the two, you see that they are not alike. Many plants crowd the sunny jungle. Plants are not as **numerous** on the rain forest floor since it is shaded by the treetops.

Today, rain forests are changing. People cut down trees and use the land to grow crops. As people **increase** their use of the land, rain forests get smaller.

We must try to protect these rain forests. Not only are they home to many animals and plants, but they also help **supply** the earth with oxygen. Rain forests give us clean air to breathe.

★ Go back to the story. Underline the words or sentences that give you a clue to the meaning of each **boldfaced** word. ★

USING CONTEXT

Meanings for the vocabulary words are given below. Go back to the story and read each sentence that has a vocabulary word. If you still cannot tell the meaning, look for clues in the sentences that come before and after the one with the vocabulary word. Write each word in front of its meaning.

thick	**increase**	**compare**	**distance**
meter	**thousand**	**supply**	**numerous**
height	**levels**		

1. ________________: many
2. ________________: how tall something is
3. ________________: to get larger in amount or size
4. ________________: a measure
5. ________________: the number 1,000
6. ________________: to give something needed
7. ________________: how far it is between things; space
8. ________________: to see how things are alike
9. ________________: having things close together
10. ________________: measures of height

CHALLENGE YOURSELF

Name two things you might measure in meters.

________________ ________________

Synonyms

Remember that **synonyms** are words that have the same or almost the same meaning. Write a word from the box that is a synonym of the underlined word in each sentence.

numerous	levels	supply	increases

1. When a tree grows, it ________________ in size.
2. So many trees and plants are in a rain forest that they are too ________________ to count.
3. Rain forests give animals a place to live and help ________________ the earth with oxygen.
4. There are three stages, or ________________, in a rain forest.

Writing Sentences

Use each vocabulary word in the box to write a sentence of your own.

distance	height	thick
thousand	compare	meter

1. ____
2. ____
3. ____
4. ____
5. ____
6. ____

WORD GAME

Write a word from the box next to each clue. Then read the words formed by the boxed letters. They name animals that live in the rain forest.

thick	thousand	distance	meter
levels	increase	supply	compare
height	numerous		

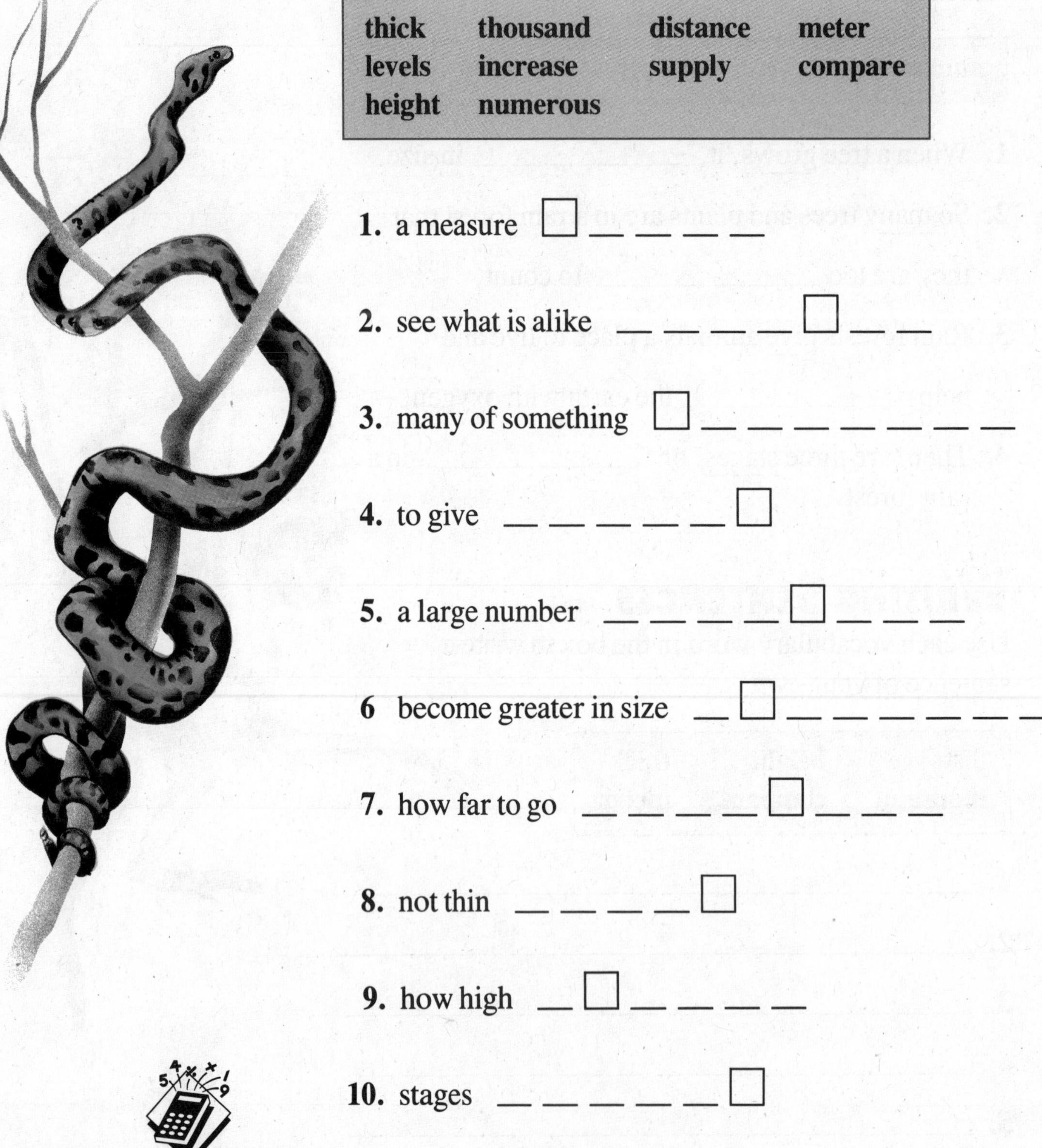

1. a measure ☐ _ _ _ _
2. see what is alike _ _ _ _ ☐ _ _
3. many of something ☐ _ _ _ _ _ _ _
4. to give _ _ _ _ _ ☐
5. a large number _ _ _ _ ☐ _ _ _
6 become greater in size _ ☐ _ _ _ _ _ _
7. how far to go _ _ _ _ ☐ _ _ _
8. not thin _ _ _ _ ☐
9. how high _ ☐ _ _ _ _
10. stages _ _ _ _ _ ☐

GET WISE TO TESTS

Directions: Find the word or words that mean the same or about the same as the boldfaced word. Mark your answer.

This test will show how well you understand the meaning of each word. Think about the meaning of the **boldfaced** word before you choose your answer.

1. a **meter** long
   Ⓐ a measure Ⓒ year
   Ⓑ amount of time Ⓓ pound
2. **increase** the amount
   Ⓕ continue Ⓗ make greater
   Ⓖ bring down Ⓙ enjoy
3. the **thick** forest
   Ⓐ crowded together Ⓒ strange
   Ⓑ thinly placed Ⓓ rich
4. **supply** food
   Ⓕ spoil Ⓗ look at
   Ⓖ throw out Ⓙ give
5. all the **levels**
   Ⓐ stars Ⓒ stages
   Ⓑ colors Ⓓ letters
6. **numerous** people
   Ⓕ some Ⓗ none
   Ⓖ many Ⓙ few
7. the tree's **height**
   Ⓐ leaves Ⓒ how tall
   Ⓑ coloring Ⓓ how heavy
8. **distance** between
   Ⓕ object Ⓗ person
   Ⓖ space Ⓙ dirt
9. **compare** things
   Ⓐ see how alike Ⓒ join
   Ⓑ complete Ⓓ leave behind
10. reached a **thousand**
    Ⓕ large number Ⓗ small child
    Ⓖ large building Ⓙ small animal

Review

1. **mosquitoes** bite
   Ⓐ flying insects Ⓒ snakes
   Ⓑ barking dogs Ⓓ children
2. brave **explorers**
   Ⓕ workers Ⓗ searchers
   Ⓖ actors Ⓙ bakers

Imagine you are on a trip through a rain forest. You can take only three pictures of what you see.

On the lines below, describe each picture you would take. Tell about the plants, animals, or insects in it. Use some vocabulary words in your writing.

Picture 1 ______

Picture 2 ______

Picture 3 ______

Turn to "My Word List" on page 131. Write some words from the story or other words that you would like to know more about. Use a dictionary to find the meanings.

★ To review the words in Lessons 1–4, turn to page 125. ★

IN THE SPOTLIGHT

The show is about to start. The room is dark. Then a single beam of light hits the stage. There in the spotlight stands the entertainer.

In Lessons 5–8, you will meet a storyteller, a dog actor, and some circus stars. They are all entertainers. They amaze us and make us laugh. Think about some performers that you have seen. What do they do to entertain others? What words describe them? Write your words under the headings below.

What Entertainers Do	**About the Entertainers**

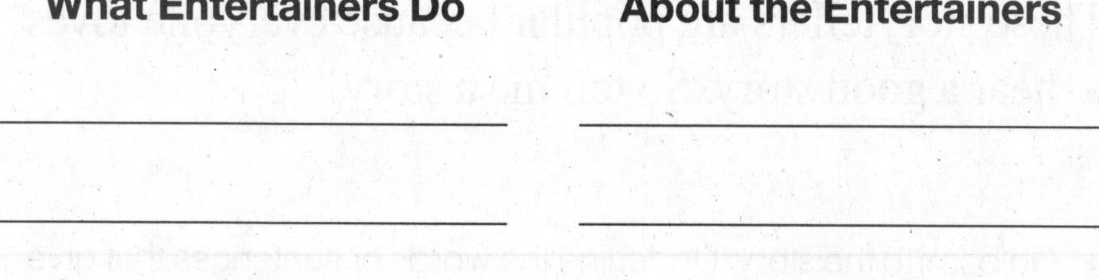

★ Read the story below. Think about the meanings of the **boldfaced** words. ★

Tell Me a Story

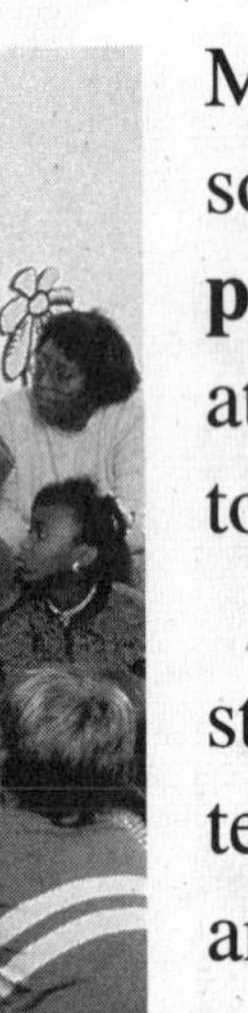

Many people tell stories just for fun. Did you know that some people make money by telling stories? These **professional** storytellers know how to hold people's attention and make them smile. They tour the country to **entertain** people in many different places.

You may have seen a storyteller at work. Some storytellers dress in a **costume** and use music to help tell a story. Seeing such a performer is a special **event**, and the storyteller wants you to enjoy it.

Author Patricia McKissack is a professional storyteller. She travels to schools and other public places to tell stories to children and adults. McKissack tells stories with power and excitement. The **energy** that she puts into her stories makes her a popular performer.

As she tells a tale, McKissack often describes a silly, **comic** character. Then the listeners burst out with **laughter** at the funny person. Just as quickly, the **audience** listens **intently** as they hear about a character in trouble. Nothing takes their attention away from the story McKissack is telling.

People have been telling stories for thousands of years. Patricia McKissack and others like her are helping to keep the **ancient** art of storytelling alive. These storytellers are popular because everyone loves to hear a good story. So tell me a story!

★ Go back to the story. Underline the words or sentences that give you a clue to the meaning of each **boldfaced** word. ★

Using Context

Meanings for the vocabulary words are given below. Go back to the story and read each sentence that has a vocabulary word. If you still cannot tell the meaning, look for clues in the sentences that come before and after the one with the vocabulary word. Write each word in front of its meaning.

ancient	**entertain**	**energy**	**comic**
professional	**audience**	**intently**	**costume**
laughter	**event**		

1. ____________________: to hold people's interest
2. ____________________: very old
3. ____________________: the power to work and act
4. ____________________: people watching a show
5. ____________________: a happening
6. ____________________: funny
7. ____________________: a special set of clothes
8. ____________________: making money by doing something that others do for fun
9. ____________________: with close attention
10. ____________________: the sound of laughing

CHALLENGE YOURSELF

Name two comic actors.

____________________ ____________________

MULTIPLE MEANINGS

The words in the boxes have more than one meaning. Look for clues in each sentence to tell which meaning is used. Write the letter of the meaning next to the correct sentence.

comic **a.** person who tells jokes; **b.** funny

1. _____ It is a comic play.
2. _____ We laughed at the comic.

entertain **a.** to hold people's attention; **b.** to have as a guest

3. _____ The story will entertain us.
4. _____ We can entertain friends at home.

CLOZE PARAGRAPH

Use the words in the box to complete the paragraph. Reread the paragraph to be sure it makes sense.

audience	**laughter**	**entertain**
event	**costume**	

Next month, we will put on a play. It is a yearly (1) ________________ that everyone enjoys. My friends and I will get to act and sing. My sister is making me a (2) ________________ to wear. It is almost finished. I can't wait to (3) ________________ all the people who will be in the (4) ________________. Our play is funny, and we want to hear their (5) ________________.

Crossword Puzzle

Use the clues and the words in the box to complete the crossword puzzle.

event	**ancient**	**costume**	**intently**
comic	**laughter**	**entertain**	
energy	**audience**	**professional**	

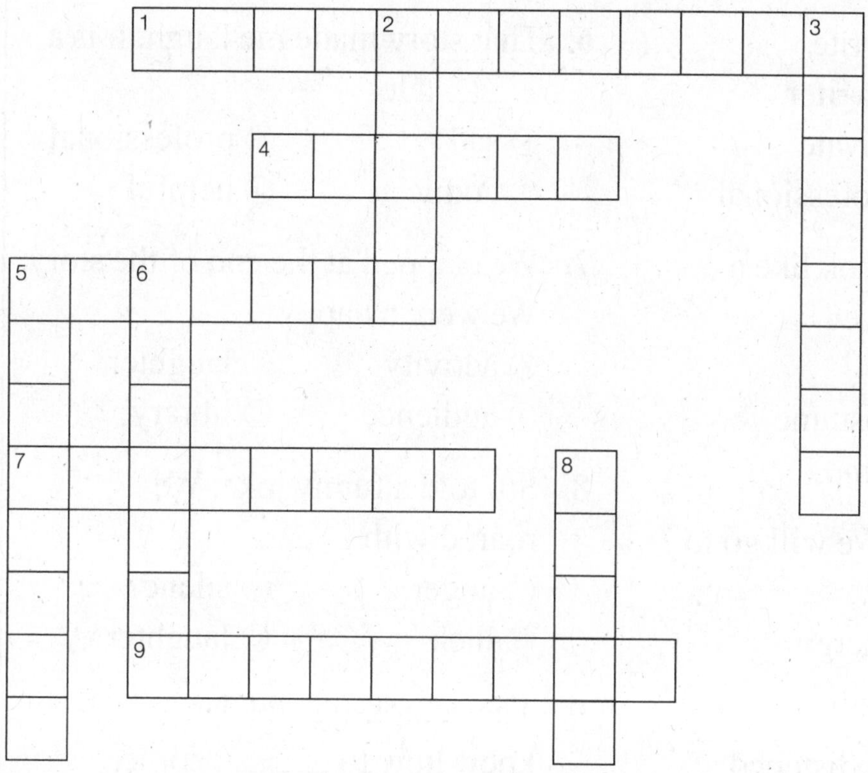

Across

1. expert
4. power to do work
5. very old
7. with great interest
9. what storytellers do

Down

2. a happening
3. sound of ha, ha, ha
5. people who listen or watch
6. special clothes for an actor or storyteller
8. funny

GET WISE TO TESTS

Directions: Fill in the space for the word that fits best in the sentence.

Read carefully. Use the other words in the sentences to help you choose each missing word.

1. Amy's son is paid to write stories. He is a _____ writer.
Ⓐ lonely Ⓒ private
Ⓑ lazy Ⓓ professional

2. Anne was dressed to look like a princess. Everyone loved her _____.
Ⓕ smile Ⓗ costume
Ⓖ dog Ⓙ lamp

3. The contest is today. We will go to see this special _____.
Ⓐ audience Ⓒ energy
Ⓑ event Ⓓ fish

4. We loved the song. We listened very _____.
Ⓕ intently Ⓗ hopefully
Ⓖ little Ⓙ sleepily

5. The museum has very old works of art. I saw an _____ vase.
Ⓐ anxious Ⓒ ancient
Ⓑ invisible Ⓓ excited

6. That story made me laugh. It is a _____ tale.
Ⓕ sad Ⓗ professional
Ⓖ comic Ⓙ helpful

7. We clapped at the end of the story. We were a happy _____.
Ⓐ activity Ⓒ laughter
Ⓑ audience Ⓓ library

8. Stu told a funny joke. We roared with _____.
Ⓕ anger Ⓗ silence
Ⓖ luck Ⓙ laughter

9. The actor sang and danced. He knew how to _____ people.
Ⓐ bore Ⓒ annoy
Ⓑ fight Ⓓ entertain

10. Ana exercises every day. She needs a lot of _____.
Ⓕ electricity Ⓗ lettuce
Ⓖ freedom Ⓙ energy

Writing

Storytellers tell different kinds of stories. They retell some old favorites. Sometimes they make up new stories. Write a story you like. It can be an old favorite or a new one. Use some vocabulary words in your writing.

Turn to "My Word List" on page 131. Write some words from the story or other words that you would like to know more about. Use a dictionary to find the meanings.

★ Read the story below. Think about the meanings of the **boldfaced** words. ★

The Ringling Brothers

This is the story of how the Ringling Brothers, growing up in McGregor, Iowa, started their famous circus in the 1800s.

The Ringling brothers woke up early in the morning on circus day. They ran down to the river to see the circus boat come in.

Al was the oldest. He was eighteen years old. Then came Gus, sixteen; Otto, twelve; Alfred Theodore, called Alf T., eight; Charlie, six; and John, who was only four. At home was Henry, the baby.

They ran after the circus band and followed along behind it. They marched in time to the music of the circus parade. Together they crowded into the tent put up for the big circus show.

All of them held their breath as a man walked a rope stretched tight above their heads. They blinked as a juggler made plates spin. They **gasped** at the riders who stood on galloping horses. When the **acrobat** turned somersaults in the air, they whistled and clapped. They laughed at the clown who tried to do it too.

For a long time after the circus had left McGregor, the sound of the wonderful calliope rang in their ears.

"What's the matter with them?" Papa Ringling wondered.

Mama Ringling rolled her eyes toward the ceiling as if it were easy to tell. "The circus is what is the matter with them," she said.

"Some day we're going to have a circus of our own," Al said. He stretched a rope over the hay in his father's barn. He began to practice tightrope walking.

They'd soon forget about the circus, their father thought. They'd all be harness **makers** one day, as he was.

"It's something they'll grow out of," Mama Ringling said hopefully.

One by one, the Ringling brothers grew into strong young men with cheerful round faces and **glossy** black hair. But they didn't **outgrow** their love for the circus.

They began to plan for a show in a ring under a Big Top. They started with the help of a real circus clown. His name was Yankee Robinson. Yankee was an old man with white whiskers. He had worked in circuses for forty years and he knew all about the circus **business**. The Ringlings made him their **partner**.

They followed his **advice** and bought **canvas** for one Big Top and one little top. They cut down trees to make center poles for the two tops. They built benches for seats under the Big Top. They bought old farm wagons, painted and decorated them, and **hired** big farm horses to pull the wagons. For a side show, they got a farmer who had taught his pig to do tricks. The pig was their only trained animal.

The new Ringling Circus opened in the town of Baraboo in May 1884.

From The Ringling Brothers, by Molly Cone

★ Go back to the story. Underline any words or sentences that give you clues to the meanings of the **boldfaced** words. ★

LITERATURE
IN THE SPOTLIGHT
LESSON 6

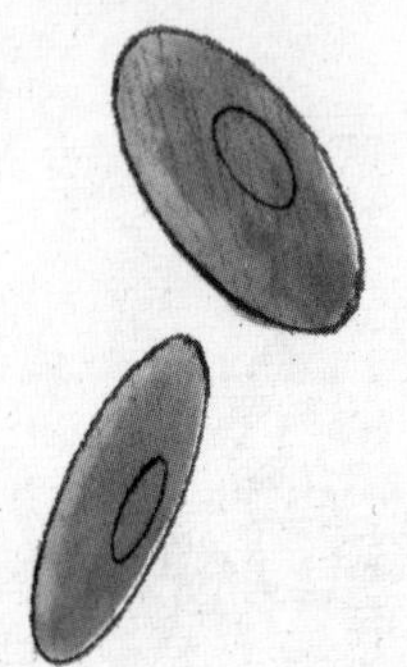

CONTEXT CLUES

Read each sentence. Look for clues to help you complete each sentence with a word from the box. Write the word on the line.

gasped	partner	glossy	outgrow
canvas	makers	acrobat	business
advice	hired		

1. The brothers went into ______________ to start a circus.
2. A man who knew about the circus became their ______________.
3. A tent was made out of ______________.
4. The benches looked shiny and ______________.
5. A friend gave them help and ______________.
6. They ______________ people to do tricks.
7. One ______________ could fly in the air.
8. The audience ______________ when they saw tricks performed.
9. Do you think people ______________ their love for the circus?
10. The ______________ of circuses answer, "No!"

CHALLENGE YOURSELF

Name two things you need to do with a partner.

______________________ ______________________

DICTIONARY SKILLS

Remember that a dictionary can help you find out how to say a word. Turn to page 133 in the Dictionary. Use the **pronunciation key** to help you learn how to say the vocabulary words in ( ) in the sentences below. Write the regular spelling for each word in ( ).

1. Listen to her (əd vīs′)! ____________________
2. I was (hīrd) yesterday. ____________________
3. The circus is my (biz′nis). ____________________
4. The surface was (glô′ sē). ____________________
5. Is that cloth (kan′vəs)? ____________________

WRITING SENTENCES

Use each vocabulary word in the box to write a sentence of your own.

makers	outgrow	gasped	partner
business	glossy	acrobat	

1. ____________________
2. ____________________
3. ____________________
4. ____________________
5. ____________________
6. ____________________
7. ____________________

GET WISE TO TESTS

Directions: Read each sentence. Pick the word that best completes the sentence. Mark the answer space for that word.

Before you choose an answer, try reading the sentence with each answer choice. This will help you choose an answer that makes sense.

1. The polished chain was _____.
Ⓐ makers Ⓒ glossy
Ⓑ happy Ⓓ silent

2. She owned a lawn care _____.
Ⓕ business Ⓗ carpenter
Ⓖ them Ⓙ canvas

3. The teacher gave the students helpful _____.
Ⓐ most Ⓒ outgrow
Ⓑ whisper Ⓓ advice

4. They _____ when the performer leaped.
Ⓕ gasped Ⓗ drown
Ⓖ hired Ⓙ more

5. Did you _____ that costume?
Ⓐ often Ⓒ slowly
Ⓑ partner Ⓓ outgrow

6. The tent was made of _____.
Ⓕ busy Ⓗ canvas
Ⓖ acrobat Ⓙ closing

7. Who are the _____ of those clown costumes?
Ⓐ mountains Ⓒ glossy
Ⓑ makers Ⓓ were

8. The _____ did three flips in a row!
Ⓕ whole Ⓗ acrobat
Ⓖ circus Ⓙ after

9. A clown was _____ to make people laugh.
Ⓐ hired Ⓒ advice
Ⓑ they Ⓓ funny

10. A new _____ often brings new ideas.
Ⓕ outgrow Ⓗ her
Ⓖ pleasing Ⓙ partner

The Ringling Brothers worked together to make their circus a success. Think about a project you have worked on with friends or family members.

Write a paragraph to tell about the group project. Name it and describe the things that you and the others did when you worked together. The pictures in the story may remind you of something. Use some vocabulary words in your writing.

Turn to "My Word List" on page 131. Write some words from the story or other words that you would like to know more about. Use a dictionary to find the meanings.

★ Read the story below. Think about the meanings of the **boldfaced** words. ★

Lights, Camera, Action!

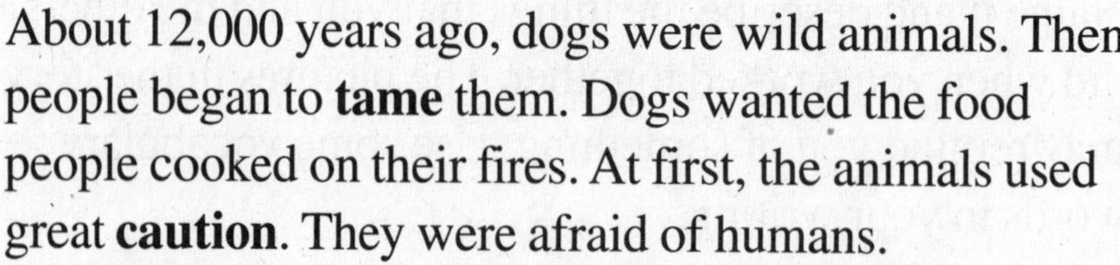

About 12,000 years ago, dogs were wild animals. Then people began to **tame** them. Dogs wanted the food people cooked on their fires. At first, the animals used great **caution**. They were afraid of humans.

As time passed, dogs **gradually** learned to trust people. People then taught dogs to help them. The dogs learned to herd sheep. People also found that they liked to have dogs around for company. Dogs became **companions** to people. Today, some people train dogs for **protection** against anyone that might try to hurt them. **Trainers** teach some dogs to guide people who cannot see. Dogs are even trained to be actors.

Becoming a good dog actor is not easy. A good dog actor must be **intelligent**. It must be smart enough to learn about 90 spoken **commands** and hand signals. You might wonder how a dog is trained to do **dangerous** things such as rescue someone from a burning building. Trainers use praise, and they repeat the commands over and over. Good dog actors catch on quickly and **respond** eagerly.

One dog trainer thinks that some dog actors really do act. Bob Weatherwax has trained many of the dogs who have played Lassie. He says that a good dog actor doesn't just follow commands. It matches the mood of the human actors. The next time you see a dog on the screen, see if you agree. Is it a dog or a real actor at work?

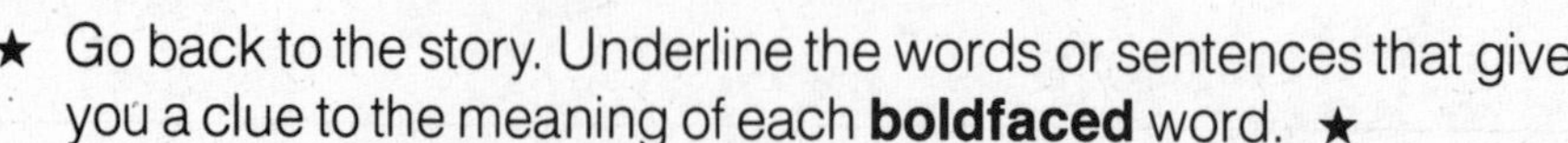

★ Go back to the story. Underline the words or sentences that give you a clue to the meaning of each **boldfaced** word. ★

USING CONTEXT

Meanings for the vocabulary words are given below. Go back to the story and read each sentence that has a vocabulary word. If you still cannot tell the meaning, look for clues in the sentences that come before and after the one with the vocabulary word. Write each word in front of its meaning.

tame	**companions**	**commands**	**caution**
gradually	**trainers**	**intelligent**	**respond**
protection	**dangerous**		

1. ________________: to act in answer to
2. ________________: people who teach animals
3. ________________: great care; interest in safety
4. ________________: something that keeps a person from harm
5. ________________: happening slowly and steadily
6. ________________: not safe
7. ________________: those who go along and keep others company; friends
8. ________________: to make a wild animal gentle and teach it to obey
9. ________________: orders or signals
10. ________________: smart

CHALLENGE YOURSELF

Name two commands you might give a dog.

________________ ________________

Cloze Paragraph

Use the words in the box to complete the paragraph. Reread the paragraph to be sure it makes sense.

commands	respond	tame
trainers	companions	gradually

Last year, we bought two dogs. We did not have to (1) ________________ the dogs, but we had to teach them to trust and obey us. Like all good (2) ________________, we gave them a lot of praise. At first, the dogs didn't (3) ________________ to our directions very well. We didn't give up, though. As the weeks passed, they ________________ learned more and more. Now they follow our (4) ________________ every time! They have turned out to be wonderful (5) ________________ and friends.

Antonyms

Remember that **antonyms** are words that have opposite meanings. Match the words in the box with the antonyms listed below. Write each word on the line.

caution
gradually
protection
dangerous
intelligent

1. safe ________________
2. stupid ________________
3. carelessness ________________
4. rapidly ________________
5. harm ________________

GET WISE TO TESTS

Directions: Fill in the space for the word or words that have the same or almost the same meaning as the boldfaced word.

Think about the meaning of the **boldfaced** word before you choose an answer. Don't be fooled by a word that looks like the **boldfaced** word.

1. **tame** dogs
   Ⓐ wash Ⓒ make gentle
   Ⓑ throw Ⓓ make wild

2. dog **trainers**
   Ⓕ teachers Ⓗ hunters
   Ⓖ pictures Ⓙ actors

3. learn **gradually**
   Ⓐ never Ⓒ rapidly
   Ⓑ bit by bit Ⓓ easily

4. **dangerous** work
   Ⓕ easy Ⓗ not safe
   Ⓖ safe Ⓙ interesting

5. **intelligent** people
   Ⓐ strong Ⓒ stupid
   Ⓑ smart Ⓓ important

6. trainer's **commands**
   Ⓕ tricks Ⓗ orders
   Ⓖ praise Ⓙ songs

7. **respond** eagerly
   Ⓐ lose Ⓒ repair
   Ⓑ answer Ⓓ rescue

8. **companions** to people
   Ⓕ gifts Ⓗ times
   Ⓖ friends Ⓙ enemies

9. for **protection**
   Ⓐ luck Ⓒ trust
   Ⓑ safety Ⓓ presents

10. use **caution**
    Ⓕ courage Ⓗ care
    Ⓖ energy Ⓙ talent

Review

1. **professional** trainer
   Ⓐ terrible Ⓒ animal.
   Ⓑ expert Ⓓ good

2. entertaining the **audience**
   Ⓕ clowns Ⓗ actors
   Ⓖ listeners Ⓙ singers

3. important **event**
   Ⓕ person Ⓗ message
   Ⓖ sleep Ⓙ happening

4. a **comic** character
   Ⓐ serious Ⓒ funny
   Ⓑ sad Ⓓ creepy

Think about what it would be like to be a dog trainer. What kinds of dogs would you like to work with? What would you want to train dogs to do? Write several sentences that tell what you think. Use the pictures to help you decide. Use some vocabulary words in your writing.

Turn to "My Word List" on page 131. Write some words from the story or other words that you would like to know more about. Use a dictionary to find the meanings.

★ Read the story below. Think about the meanings of the **boldfaced** words. ★

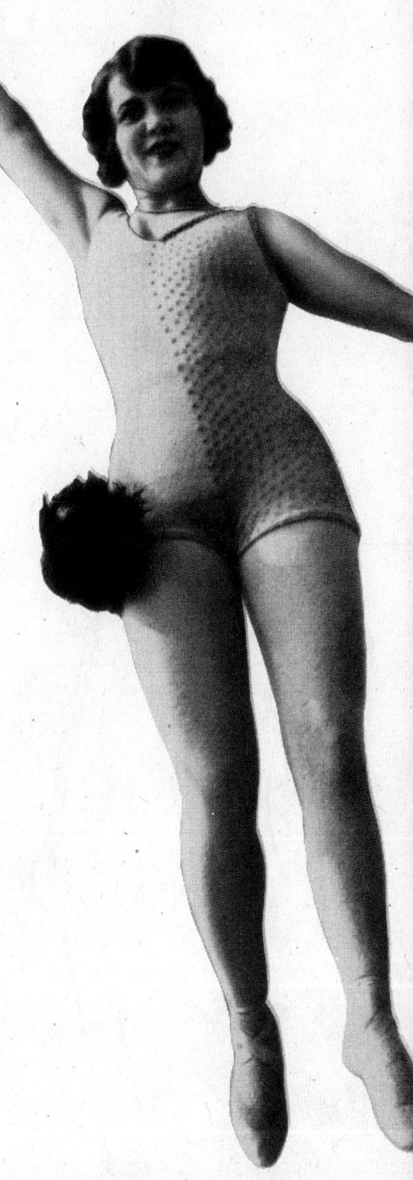

The Spinning Star

The lights go down. Heads look up. At the top of the tent a woman spins around on metal loops attached to ropes. The **performer** is Lillian Leitzel, a circus star.

In her time (1891-1931), Leitzel was one of the world's most famous circus performers. She had a very **difficult** act, but she made it look easy. Leitzel had **confidence** in her skills. She believed in what she could do, and so did her fans.

To begin her act, Leitzel went up a long rope that hung from the top of the tent. Her trip up the rope was done in a series of smooth, **graceful** movements. She spun by swinging from hand to hand and turning her body over each time she changed hands. To do this, Leitzel had to be very strong and in good **condition**. The big **muscles** in her arms and shoulders helped.

At the top of the rope, far above the crowd, Lillian Leitzel did handstands and other **balancing** tricks. Then came the hardest part, her biggest **challenge**. She held onto a metal ring with one hand. Then she swung her body up and over the ring again and again. Leitzel did this **exhausting** trick at least 75 times a show. Only an **athlete** in top condition could do this.

In 1931, a ring Leitzel was using broke during one of her acts. She fell to her death. It was a great loss to the circus world. But Lillian Leitzel will always be remembered for her bravery and skill.

★ Go back to the story. Underline the words or sentences that give you a clue to the meaning of each **boldfaced** word. ★

HEALTH
IN THE SPOTLIGHT
LESSON 8

Context Clues

Read each sentence. Look for clues to help you complete each sentence with a word or words from the box. Write the word on the line.

confidence	**challenge**	**graceful**	**balancing**
performer	**muscles**	**difficult**	**exhausting**
condition	**athlete**		

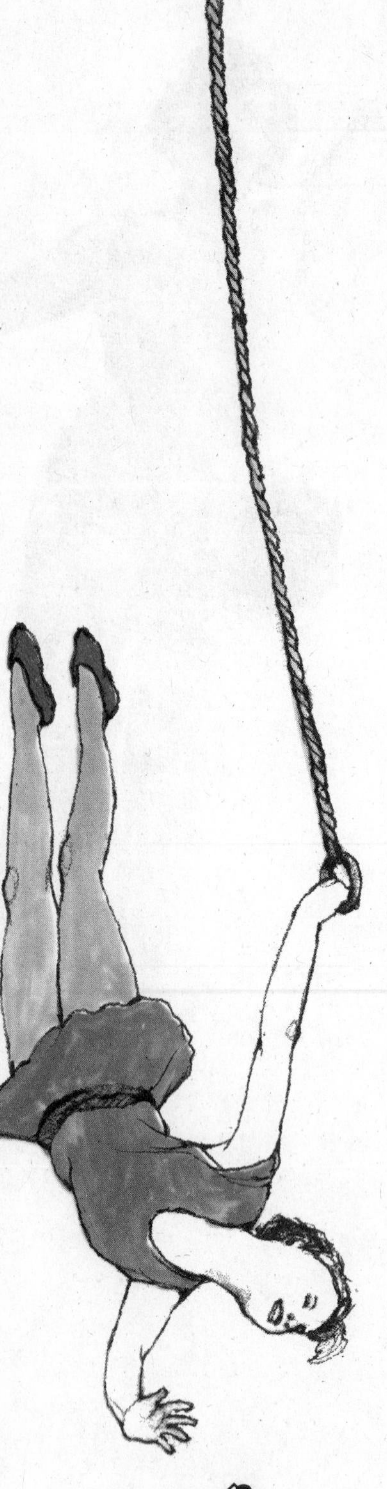

1. Like a swimmer, runner, or other ________________, Lillian Leitzel practiced a lot.
2. Practice helped her learn ________________ tricks, like ________________ on a rope.
3. She also exercised to stay in good ________________.
4. Leitzel needed strong arm ________________.
5. Her movements had to be smooth and ________________.
6. She also needed ________________, or belief, in herself.
7. For Lillian Leitzel, doing hard tricks was a ____________.
8. The life of a circus ________________ was exciting.
9. But the long days of tiring work were also ____________.

Synonyms

Remember that **synonyms** are words that have the same or almost the same meaning. Match the words in the box with their synonyms. Write each word on the line.

difficult	athlete	exhausting	confidence

1. tiring ______________________
2. trust ______________________
3. hard ______________________
4. runner ______________________

Dictionary Skills

A dictionary gives the meanings of words. Turn to the Dictionary, which begins on page 133. Find each word in the Dictionary. Write its meaning below.

1. graceful: ______________________
2. challenge: ______________________
3. performer: ______________________
4. balancing: ______________________
5. condition: ______________________
6. muscles: ______________________
7. confidence: ______________________
8. exhausting: ______________________
9. athlete: ______________________

HEALTH
IN THE SPOTLIGHT
LESSON 8

WORD MAP

Words can be put on a kind of map to show what they have in common. Write each word from the box in the group where it belongs to tell about Lillian Leitzel.

confidence	**challenges**	**graceful**	**balancing**
performer	**muscles**	**difficult**	**exhausting**
condition	**athlete**		

What She Is

a ________________

an ________________

What She Has

body ________________

________________ in herself

LILLIAN LEITZEL

What She Faces

big ________________

________________ work

What Kind of Tricks She Does

________________ tricks

________________ acts

What She Has to Be

very ________________

in good ________________

GET WISE TO TESTS

Directions: Read each sentence. Pick the word that best completes the sentence. Mark the answer space for that word.

Before you choose an answer, try reading the sentence with each answer choice. This will help you choose an answer that makes sense.

1. A circus _____ appears in front of many people.
   Ⓐ play Ⓑ crying Ⓒ performer Ⓓ lazy

2. A _____ act takes skill.
   Ⓕ looking Ⓖ balancing Ⓗ cause Ⓙ face

3. This circus work is _____.
   Ⓐ door Ⓑ difficult Ⓒ laughing Ⓓ they

4. She has strong _____.
   Ⓕ muscles Ⓖ athlete Ⓗ tired Ⓙ it

5. Watch her _____ movements.
   Ⓐ challenge Ⓑ lost Ⓒ graceful Ⓓ roasted

6. I have had an _____ day.
   Ⓕ note Ⓖ exhausting Ⓗ muscles Ⓙ wish

7. We have _____ in you.
   Ⓐ balancing Ⓑ confidence Ⓒ helpful Ⓓ also

8. You are in good _____.
   Ⓕ condition Ⓖ graceful Ⓗ cost Ⓙ happy

9. Here is our star _____.
   Ⓐ after Ⓑ away Ⓒ athlete Ⓓ most

10. This is a big _____.
    Ⓕ please Ⓖ difficult Ⓗ challenge Ⓙ exhausting

Review

1. A _____ lion is not safe.
   Ⓐ jumped Ⓑ dangerous Ⓒ easily Ⓓ they

2. Trained animals _____ quickly.
   Ⓕ respond Ⓖ happy Ⓗ our Ⓙ hunter

When a circus comes to town, it puts up ads to get people to come to the show. Each ad describes the acts and performers. Imagine that you have a circus. Your circus has different kinds of performers and animals.

Write your own ad. Tell why your circus is the best circus and why people should buy a ticket to see it. Use some vocabulary words in your writing.

CIRCUS

Come one, come all, to the greatest circus on Earth! You will see ______________________

____

____

____

____

____

____

____

____

____

Turn to "My Word List" on page 131. Write some words from the story or other words that you would like to know more about. Use a dictionary to find the meanings.

★ To review the words in Lessons 5–8, turn to page 126. ★

Imaginary Characters

Your favorite stories and shows may be about imaginary characters. Even though they are not real, they often remind us of people in the real world.

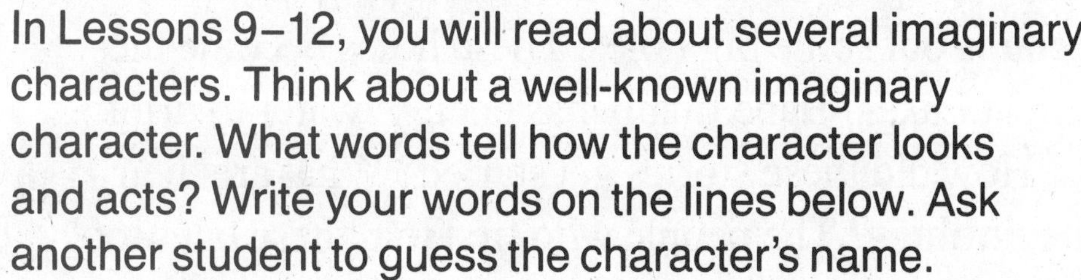

In Lessons 9–12, you will read about several imaginary characters. Think about a well-known imaginary character. What words tell how the character looks and acts? Write your words on the lines below. Ask another student to guess the character's name.

About My Character's Looks	**About My Character's Actions**
____________________	____________________
____________________	____________________
____________________	____________________

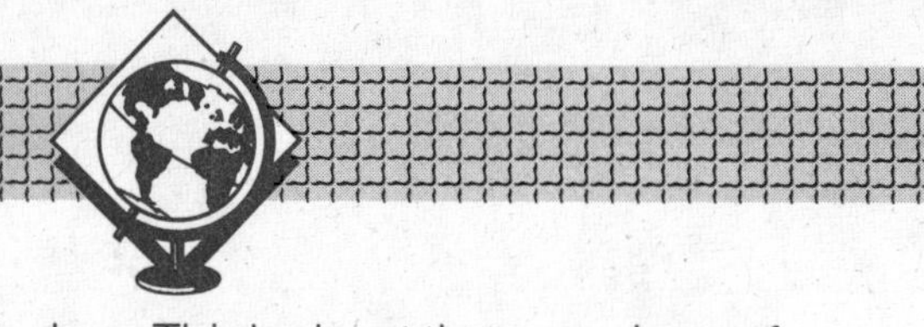

★ Read the story below. Think about the meanings of the **boldfaced** words. ★

Mighty Paul Bunyan

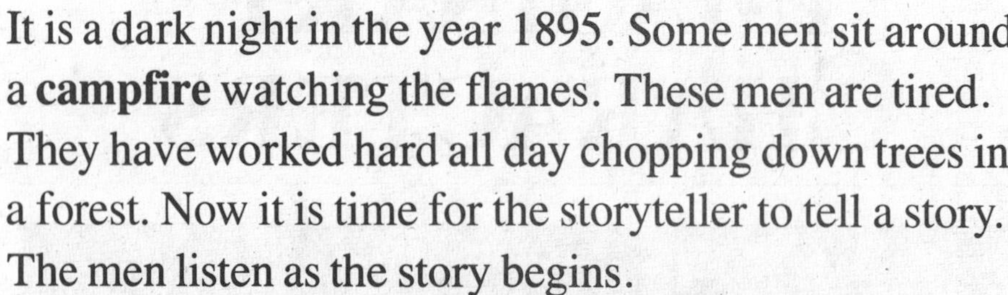

It is a dark night in the year 1895. Some men sit around a **campfire** watching the flames. These men are tired. They have worked hard all day chopping down trees in a forest. Now it is time for the storyteller to tell a story. The men listen as the story begins.

This **tale** is about a mighty man called Paul Bunyan. Paul is a lumberjack just like the men around the fire. He, too, chops down trees in the **wilderness**, far away from other people. But Paul Bunyan is not a real person. He is **imaginary**. He is bigger and stronger than real men and can do much more work. Paul Bunyan has the **ability** to clear a whole forest by himself! He eats more than real men do, too. It takes a whole **orchard** of trees to get enough apples to make him a pie!

Paul has a giant blue ox named Babe. Paul and Babe do many exciting things and have many **adventures**. For example, when Babe needs drinking water, Paul **scoops** out some big holes. These holes become the Great Lakes. Babe finally has enough water to drink!

How did these stories get started? What are their **beginnings**? The people who first told these tales took pride in their work as lumberjacks. This was their way of showing it. Over the years, these **legends** got passed along, and then were written down. Today, Paul Bunyan still stands for the kind of men and women who made our country strong.

★ Go back to the story. Underline the words or sentences that give you a clue to the meaning of each **boldfaced** word. ★

Context Clues

Read each sentence. Look for clues to help you complete each sentence with a word or words from the box. Write the word on the line.

campfire	scoops	imaginary	tale
ability	wilderness	beginnings	legends
orchard	adventures		

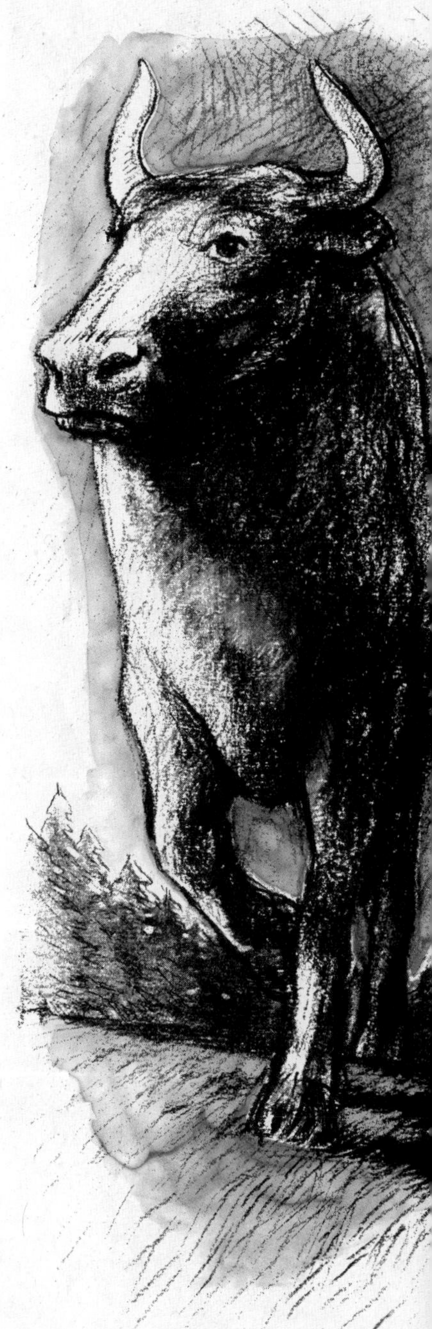

1. Everyone outside was warmed by the ________________.
2. They listened to a ________________ told by a talented storyteller.
3. Paul Bunyan, an ________________ person, lived in the ________________ areas of America.
4. He had the ________________ to chop down a whole ________________ of trees at once.
5. In some of the stories, or ________________, that people tell, Paul is helped by a blue ox named Babe.
6. In one of their exciting ________________, Paul ________________ out holes and makes the Great Lakes.
7. These stories had their ________________ about a hundred years ago.

CHALLENGE YOURSELF

Name two imaginary characters in books you have read.

________________ ________________

DICTIONARY SKILLS

Answer the questions below. Use the Dictionary if you need help.

1. How is a legend like a tale? ______________________
2. Which means "power to do something": ability or adventures? ______________________
3. Which means "unusual experiences": adventures or scoops? ______________________
4. What would you find in both an orchard and the wilderness? ______________________
5. What would you do with a campfire? ______________________

WRITING SENTENCES

Use each vocabulary word in the box to write a sentence of your own.

beginnings	legends	imaginary
adventures	campfire	wilderness

1. ______________________
2. ______________________
3. ______________________
4. ______________________
5. ______________________
6. ______________________

Tangled-up Words

A word is underlined in each sentence below. The word sounds something like a word in the box. But its meaning makes it the wrong word for the sentence.

Read the paragraphs. Find the word in the box that can replace the underlined word. Write the vocabulary word on the line next to the number of the underlined word.

adventures	**legends**	**campfires**	**tale**
scoops	**orchard**	**wilderness**	**imaginary**
beginnings	**ability**		

Paul Bunyan is an (1) ordinary character. Storytellers often tell stories about him. These stories are told around (2) cameras. One (3) tail is about how much Paul can eat. It takes a whole (4) orange of apples to make him a pie. Another story is about some holes he (5) scares out for Babe. They become the Great Lakes!

There are many other (6) ledges about Paul and his blue ox, Babe. Most tell about their different (7) alligators in the (8) windowsill.

People enjoy learning about the (9) buildings of a country through stories. Some people have a great (10) enemy to tell these stories well.

1. ________________
2. ________________
3. ________________
4. ________________
5. ________________
6. ________________
7. ________________
8. ________________
9. ________________
10. ________________

Get Wise to Tests

Directions: Read each sentence carefully. Then choose the best answer to complete each sentence. Mark the space for the answer you have chosen.

If you are not sure which word completes the sentence, do the best you can. Try to choose the answer that makes the most sense.

1. A **tale** is a kind of _____.
   Ⓐ story Ⓒ dog
   Ⓑ character Ⓓ poem

2. A **campfire** is built in the _____.
   Ⓕ stove Ⓗ woods
   Ⓖ vans Ⓙ city

3. A person who **scoops** out dirt _____ it out.
   Ⓐ digs Ⓒ fills
   Ⓑ washes Ⓓ blows

4. A **wilderness** is a _____ place.
   Ⓕ tasty Ⓗ space
   Ⓖ city Ⓙ wild

5. An **imaginary** story is _____.
   Ⓐ true Ⓒ old
   Ⓑ not real Ⓓ short

6. Someone with **ability** has _____.
   Ⓕ instruments Ⓗ charm
   Ⓖ skill Ⓙ wrinkles

7. An **orchard** has many _____.
   Ⓐ children Ⓒ trees
   Ⓑ animals Ⓓ rooms

8. **Adventures** are _____.
   Ⓕ exciting Ⓗ proud
   Ⓖ dull Ⓙ messy

9. **Beginnings** are how something was _____.
   Ⓐ written Ⓒ won
   Ⓑ finished Ⓓ started

10. **Legends** are well-known _____.
    Ⓕ recipes Ⓗ heroes
    Ⓖ stories Ⓙ accidents

Review

1. A **difficult** job is _____ to do.
   Ⓐ soft Ⓒ hard
   Ⓑ lazy Ⓓ easy

2. An **athlete** is good at _____ .
   Ⓕ shopping Ⓗ cooking
   Ⓖ drawing Ⓙ sports

Writing

Look at the picture. Pretend you are Paul Bunyan. You have just met someone bigger and stronger than you are.

Describe the new character and tell how you feel about her. The picture will give you ideas. Use some vocabulary words in your writing.

I was walking through the forest when, to my surprise, I saw ______________________________

Turn to "My Word List" on page 132. Write some words from the story or other words that you would like to know more about. Use a dictionary to find the meanings.

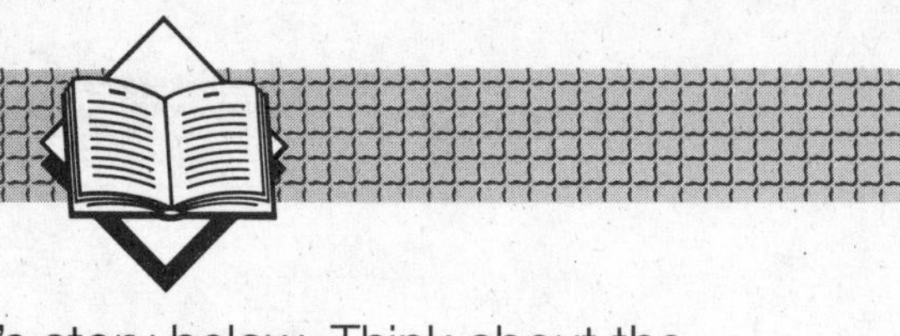

★ Read the children's story below. Think about the meanings of the **boldfaced** words. ★

How Spider Got a Thin Waist

This story tells how Spider came to have such a tiny waist.

One day Spider was walking through the forest. It was early morning and he noticed an **unusually** pleasant smell. It was food! Today was the festival of the harvest. Every village in the big forest was preparing a **feast**. The women were cooking **yams** and cassava, and chicken with peanut-flavored sauce.

Spider's heart jumped for joy. His mouth watered. His eyes **sparkled** and he smiled brightly.

Now, of course, Spider had not done any of the work to deserve such a feast, and no one had invited him to come and eat. All day he played in the sun or slept, and since it is not the **custom** to **refuse** food to anyone who comes to one's door, he could eat very well by **simply** visiting all his friends.

Now Spider was right in the middle of the forest. Not far away there were two villages. Spider stood just in the middle, and the two were exactly the same distance away. Today each village would have a great feast.

Since there were two dinners, he did not know which one he wanted to go to. At last he had an idea! He could go to them both! Of course. Spider was so pleased with his good idea that he did a little dance right there and then.

But how could he know when the food was ready? And then he had another idea. He did another little dance just because he was so **brilliant**. And then he did two things.

First, he called his eldest son, Kuma. He took a long rope and tied one end around his **waist**. The other end he gave to his son.

"Take this rope to the village on the East," he said to Kuma. "When the food is ready, give the rope a hard pull, and I will know it is time for me to come and eat."

Then Spider called his youngest son, Kwaku. He took another long rope and tied it around his waist, just below the first one.

"Kwaku, take this rope to the village on the West," he said, "and when the food is all cooked, pull very hard on it. Then I will come and have my fill."

My friends, can you imagine what happened? I don't think so, so I will tell you. The people in the East village and the people in the West village had their dinners at *exactly the same time*.

Kuma and Kwaku could not understand why their father did not come, and they pulled harder all the time. And something was happening to Spider. The ropes **squeezed** tighter and tighter and his waist got thinner and thinner. Kuma and Kwaku waited until all the food was eaten. Then they came to look for their father. When they found him, he looked very different. His waistline was thinner than a needle! Spider never grew fat again. He stayed the same until today. He has a big head and a big body, and a tiny little waist in between.

From The Adventures of Spider: West African Folk Tales, retold by Joyce Cooper Arkhurst

★ Go back to the story. Underline any words or sentences that give you clues to the meanings of the **boldfaced** words. ★

Context Clues

Read each sentence. Look for clues to help you complete each sentence with a word from the box. Write the word on the line.

brilliant	simply	sparkled	feast
unusually	waist	custom	yams
squeezed	refuse		

1. Spider enjoyed eating ____________, or sweet potatoes, and most other kinds of food.
2. When he smelled food cooking, his eyes opened wide and ____________ brightly.
3. Spider knew that the people in two nearby villages were cooking food for a ____________.
4. He knew that he could get food just by going to the village and ____________ being there.
5. He knew his friends would not ____________ to share their food with him, for they were kind.
6. He was glad it was the ____________, or usual way of doing things, to give food to visitors.
7. Spider did not often eat two feasts in one day, but he was ____________ hungry this day.
8. He had a ____________, or clever, plan.
9. He tied two ropes around his ____________, or middle.
10. The plan failed, and the ropes ____________ his body instead of telling him when he could eat!

ANTONYMS

Antonyms are words that have opposite meanings. Match the words in the box with their antonyms listed below. Write each word on the line.

unusually	refuse	brilliant

1. accept ________________
2. dumb ________________
3. usually ________________

CLOZE PARAGRAPH

Use the words in the box to complete the paragraph. Reread the paragraph to be sure it makes sense.

Yams	feast	sparkled	simply
custom	squeezed	waist	

Spider depended on the (1) ________________ of giving food to visitors. He hoped to eat at a (2) ________________ without helping to prepare it. (3) ________________ were one of his favorite foods. His eyes (4) ________________ brightly when he thought of them. But it was his love of food that got Spider a thin (5) ________________. If he had (6) ________________ gone to one feast, instead of trying to go to two, his waist probably would not have been (7) ________________ so hard.

GET WISE TO TESTS

Directions: Read each sentence. Pick the word that best completes the sentence. Mark the answer space for that word.

Before you choose an answer, try reading the sentence with each answer choice. This will help you choose an answer that makes sense.

1. It is the _____ in that country to bow to people you meet.
Ⓐ refuse Ⓒ idea
Ⓑ custom Ⓓ away

2. I know we will _____ to get the children another dog.
Ⓕ liking Ⓗ refuse
Ⓖ simply Ⓙ forget

3. It is an _____ cold day for this time of year.
Ⓐ simply Ⓒ extreme
Ⓑ unusually Ⓓ icing

4. We celebrate most holidays with a _____ of good foods.
Ⓕ feast Ⓗ yams
Ⓖ customs Ⓙ cheer

5. If you would _____ ask me, I could easily tell you what I would like for my birthday.
Ⓐ about Ⓒ simply
Ⓑ happy Ⓓ hardly

6. She thought her idea was good, but I thought it was _____.
Ⓕ sparkled Ⓗ unusually
Ⓖ slowly Ⓙ brilliant

7. The gold _____ in the sun.
Ⓐ squeezed Ⓒ danced
Ⓑ sparkled Ⓓ melting

8. I love Thanksgiving dinner because it is the one meal when I know we will have _____ to eat.
Ⓕ yams Ⓗ dress
Ⓖ feast Ⓙ nothing

9. I have been exercising to try to slim down my _____.
Ⓐ toes Ⓒ custom
Ⓑ health Ⓓ waist

10. The juice I am drinking came from oranges that were _____.
Ⓕ squeezed Ⓗ freshly
Ⓖ brilliant Ⓙ picking

Think of someone else who has wanted to get something without working for it. It might be a real person or someone in a story.

Write a paragraph explaining how this person acted like Spider. Tell what happened because of the way this person acted. Use some vocabulary words in your writing.

Turn to "My Word List" on page 132. **Write some words from the story or other words that you would like to know more about. Use a dictionary to find the meanings.**

★ Read the story below. Think about the meanings of the **boldfaced** words. ★

The Mickey Mouse Man

Have you ever been to Disney World or to Disneyland? If you have, then you know who Walt Disney was. He made his living in the **entertainment** business. Or, you could say his **career** was amusing people. One way Disney did this was by inventing animal **characters** such as Mickey Mouse and Donald Duck.

When he was a boy, Walt Disney liked to draw. At the age of 16, he began to study art in Chicago, Illinois. His **drawings** showed that he was a good artist. He had **talent**.

Six years later, Disney moved to California to make **cartoons**. A cartoon is a movie made from thousands of drawings. Each one shows a small part of the character's actions.

Disney set up a **studio** so he would have a place to make his movies. His first cartoon was about Mickey Mouse. People were **delighted** with Mickey Mouse. They loved his big ears and were **enchanted** with his squeaky voice. (They did not know it was really Walt Disney's own charming voice!)

Walt Disney went on to make many other cartoons. People liked the **humor** in Disney's cartoons. The stories were funny, and the characters did silly things.

Today, the Disney Studios still carry on Walt Disney's work. Mickey Mouse and the other Disney characters still make people laugh.

★ Go back to the story. Underline the words or sentences that give you a clue to the meaning of each **boldfaced** word. ★

Using Context

Meanings for the vocabulary words are given below. Go back to the story and read each sentence that has a vocabulary word. If you still cannot tell the meaning, look for clues in the sentences that come before and after the one with the vocabulary word. Write each word in front of its meaning.

characters	**career**	**drawings**	**talent**
entertainment	**studio**	**delighted**	**humor**
cartoons	**enchanted**		

1. ______________: a person's life work
2. ______________: place where an artist might work
3. ______________: pictures done with pencil, pen, or crayon
4. ______________: very pleased and happy
5. ______________: something that keeps people interested
6. ______________: movies made from many pictures
7. ______________: greatly charmed
8. ______________: people and animals in a story
9. ______________: what makes someone laugh
10. ______________: special ability

FINE ARTS
IMAGINARY CHARACTERS
LESSON 11

Classifying

Each column groups words about Walt Disney. Write each word from the box in the group where it belongs.

cartoons	characters	enchanted
drawings	delighted	

WALT DISNEY

What He Created Himself	How He Made People Feel
______________	______________
______________	______________
______________	

Writing Sentences

Use each vocabulary word in the box to write a sentence of your own.

humor	talent	entertainment
career	studio	characters

1. ______________________________
2. ______________________________
3. ______________________________
4. ______________________________
5. ______________________________
6. ______________________________

GET WISE TO TESTS

Directions: Read the phrase. Look for the word or words that have the same or almost the same meaning as the boldfaced word. Mark the letter for your choice.

Always read all the answer choices. Many choices may make sense. But only one answer choice has the same or almost the same meaning as the **boldfaced** word.

1. Disney **cartoons**
   Ⓐ car tools Ⓒ coats
   Ⓑ plays Ⓓ movies

2. person's **career**
   Ⓕ life's work Ⓗ drawings
   Ⓖ name Ⓙ hobby

3. Disney **characters**
   Ⓐ actions Ⓒ animals or people
   Ⓑ charms Ⓓ candies

4. artist's **studio**
   Ⓕ student Ⓗ idea
   Ⓖ brush Ⓙ place of work

5. box of **drawings**
   Ⓐ books Ⓒ pictures
   Ⓑ letters Ⓓ paints

6. with **humor**
   Ⓕ love Ⓗ hate
   Ⓖ fun Ⓙ tears

7. good **entertainment**
   Ⓐ creepy thing Ⓒ empty thing
   Ⓑ silly thing Ⓓ interesting thing

8. having **talent**
   Ⓕ ability Ⓗ beauty
   Ⓖ attention Ⓙ business

9. become **enchanted**
   Ⓐ cheerful Ⓒ surprised
   Ⓑ charmed Ⓓ eaten

10. feel **delighted**
    Ⓕ unhappy Ⓗ curious
    Ⓖ pleased Ⓙ deserted

Review

1. good **beginnings**
   Ⓐ starts Ⓒ beings
   Ⓑ stops Ⓓ ideas

2. **imaginary** person
   Ⓕ happy Ⓗ not real
   Ⓖ real Ⓙ important

Pretend that you have been asked to create a brand-new cartoon character for a movie. Write a paragraph describing your character. What is its name? How does it look? Use some vocabulary words in your writing.

Turn to "My Word List" on page 132. Write some words from the story or other words that you would like to know more about. Use a dictionary to find the meanings.

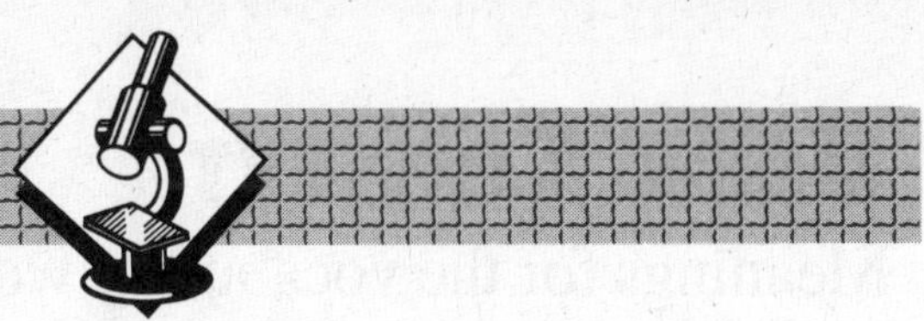

★ Read the story below. Think about the meanings of the **boldfaced** words. ★

Computer Cartoons

When you turn on your **television** set, you can almost always find a cartoon. The cartoon may be a show like Bugs Bunny. Or it may be a **commercial** to help sell a toy. You can even see whole movies that are cartoons. They are fun for us to watch. But for many years, **creating** cartoons was hard work. To make cartoons, artists had to draw **countless** pictures by hand. Then the artists had to **arrange** the thousands of pictures from the beginning of the cartoon to the end.

Today, computers are making the job of cartoon artists much easier. First, the artists use the computer to draw the shape of an object or person. This **figure** looks like a wire sculpture. The computer lets the artists look at the figure from any direction – front, back, top, or bottom. The artists use the keyboard or mouse to turn the figure and make it move. The artists then **develop** the figure. For example, they add face details such as hair, a nose, mouth, and eyes. They also add clothes to the figure.

To show a **motion** such as skipping, computer artists only have to draw pictures of the figure at the beginning, middle, and end of the movement. The computer then fills in the **images** in between because it has a record of how the figure looks when it moves. The **effect** is smooth movement that looks real and a cartoon character that is a modern work of art.

★ Go back to the story. Underline the words or sentences that give you a clue to the meaning of each **boldfaced** word. ★

SCIENCE
IMAGINARY CHARACTERS
LESSON 12

USING CONTEXT

Meanings for the vocabulary words are given below. Go back to the story and read each sentence that has a vocabulary word. If you still cannot tell the meaning, look for clues in the sentences that come before and after the one with the vocabulary word. Write each word in front of its meaning.

figure	**countless**	**develop**	**motion**
television	**creating**	**images**	**commercial**
arrange	**effect**		

1. ____________: likenesses of people, animals, or things
2. ____________: to work out in detail
3. ____________: a machine that shows pictures with sounds
4. ____________: the act of moving
5. ____________: an ad on the radio or television
6. ____________: too many to be counted
7. ____________: to put in some kind of order
8. ____________: a shape
9. ____________: the act of making something new
10. ____________: the result

Cloze Paragraph

Use the words in the box to complete the paragraph. Reread the paragraph to be sure it makes sense.

countless	television	creating	commercial

Last night I turned on the (1) _______________ set. I was looking for a cartoon movie. As I flipped through the channels, I saw a great (2) _______________. It was an ad for the new science museum. An artist had painted (3) _______________ pictures of insects all over the walls of the museum. I'll bet that (4) _______________ all those pictures took him months!

Multiple Meanings

The words in the box have more than one meaning. Look for clues in each sentence to tell which meaning is being used. Write the letter of the meaning next to the correct sentence.

develop	figures
a. to work out in detail	**a.** numbers
b. to make bigger or better	**b.** shapes

_____ **1.** Exercise helped him develop his muscles.

_____ **2.** We will develop her idea for the cartoon.

_____ **3.** We added the figures in the math problem.

_____ **4.** Some figures on the screen look like people.

SCIENCE
IMAGINARY CHARACTERS
LESSON 12

DICTIONARY SKILLS

Remember that **guide words** are the two words at the top of each dictionary page. They show the first and last words on a page. All the words in between are in ABC order. Decide which words from the box would go on each page. Write the words in ABC order.

effect	countless	figure
commercial	develop	creating

camel/cup	day/forget

CLASSIFYING

Each column groups words about computer artists. Write each word from the box in the group where it belongs.

commercial	images	develop
arrange	figure	

What Artists Do	What Artists Can Make

GET WISE TO TESTS

Directions: Read each sentence carefully. Then choose the best answer to complete each sentence. Mark the letter of the answer you have chosen.

Some tests have letters in the answer circles. Fill in the circle next to your answer. Be sure to cover the letter, too.

1. If you want to get people to buy something, you can write a _____.
Ⓐ copy Ⓑ model Ⓒ book Ⓓ commercial

2. Numbers and shapes are _____.
Ⓕ fingers Ⓖ places Ⓗ names Ⓙ figures

3. You can watch movies, sports events, and news on a _____.
Ⓐ radio Ⓑ stereo Ⓒ television Ⓓ telephone

4. Today, _____ cartoons is easier than it used to be.
Ⓕ watching Ⓖ crushing Ⓗ helping Ⓙ creating

5. Computer artists make _____ that move on the screen.
Ⓐ ideas Ⓑ wires Ⓒ images Ⓓ keyboards

6. Before computers, artists had to draw _____ pictures by hand.
Ⓕ some Ⓖ countless Ⓗ few Ⓙ fifteen

7. When something moves, it is in _____.
Ⓐ motor Ⓑ television Ⓒ motion Ⓓ comments

8. If you work out an idea in detail, you _____ it.
Ⓕ deliver Ⓖ expect Ⓗ leave Ⓙ develop

9. When you put things in order, you _____ them.
Ⓐ arrange Ⓑ open Ⓒ keep Ⓓ protect

10. The result of something that you make happen is an _____.
Ⓕ effect Ⓖ effort Ⓗ audience Ⓙ information

Review

1. **Drawings** are _____.
Ⓐ colors Ⓑ student Ⓒ pictures Ⓓ hobby

2. A **career** is a _____.
Ⓕ life's work Ⓖ animals Ⓗ road Ⓙ letters

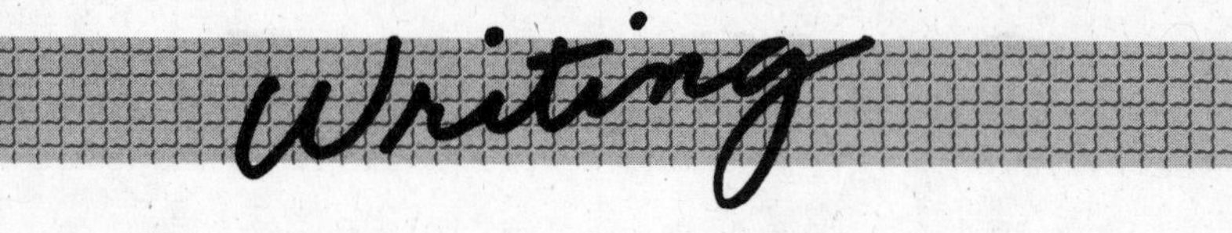

Many commercials are cartoons. What kind of cartoon commercial would you create to get people to go to your favorite restaurant or buy your favorite snack food?

Turn to "My Word List" on page 132. Write some words from the story or other words that you would like to know more about. Use a dictionary to find the meanings.

★ To review the words in Lessons 9–12, turn to page 127. ★

WATER EVERYWHERE

The sea around us is another world. This world of large and small creatures and buried treasure invites us to explore.

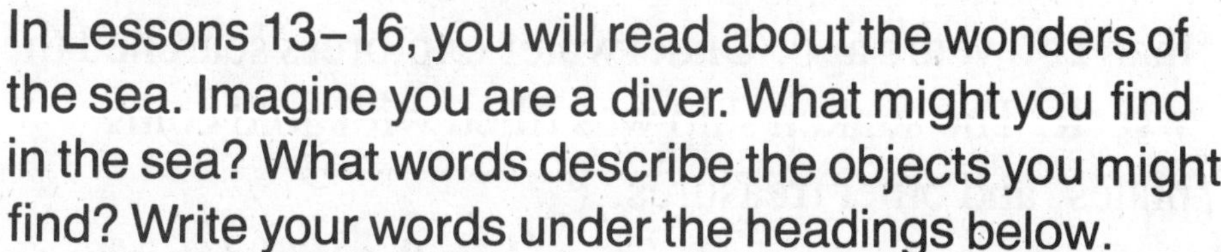

In Lessons 13–16, you will read about the wonders of the sea. Imagine you are a diver. What might you find in the sea? What words describe the objects you might find? Write your words under the headings below.

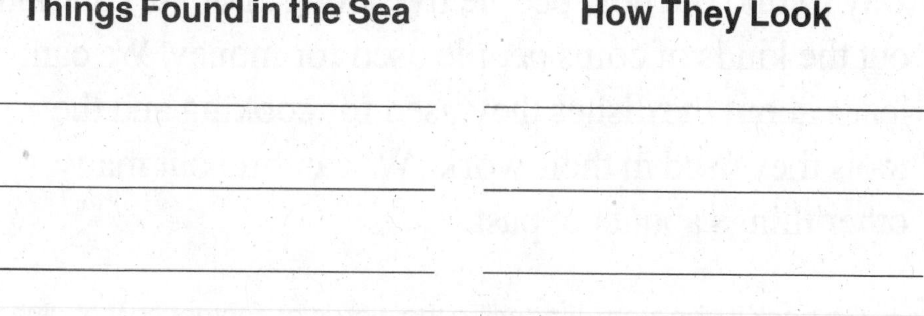

Things Found in the Sea	How They Look
______________________	______________________
______________________	______________________
______________________	______________________
______________________	______________________

★ Read the story below. Think about the meanings of the **boldfaced** words. ★

Treasure Under the Sea

In the old days, many ships sailed the seas. The ships' tall, wooden **masts** held up giant sails to catch the wind. The largest of these **sailboats** carried more than 400 men. Many of these boats were **trade** ships loaded with things that people would buy, such as tea, silk, spices, and gold. This **cargo** put the ships in danger from **pirates**.

Pirate ships roamed the sea searching for ships to attack. They hoped to steal gold, silver, and other **treasures**. When pirates attacked, the **sailors** who worked on the ship would fight to protect the cargo. Sometimes a ship would sink during a fight, taking the men, or **crew**, and the treasure with it.

In 1982, **divers** found a pirate ship named *Whydah*. The old sailing ship was found off the coast of Massachusetts. It sank to the bottom of the sea more than 250 years ago. Underwater explorers searched the **wreck**. The sunken ship was filled with gold coins, plates, and other treasures.

Exploring old wrecks at sea like the *Whydah* is one way to find out how people lived long ago. We can find out the kinds of coins people used for money. We can learn about the dishes they used for cooking and the tools they used in their work. We can find out many other things about the past.

★ Go back to the story. Underline the words or sentences that give you a clue to the meaning of each **boldfaced** word. ★

USING CONTEXT

Meanings for the vocabulary words are given below. Go back to the story and read each sentence that has a vocabulary word. If you still cannot tell the meaning, look for clues in the sentences that come before and after the one with the vocabulary word Write each word in front of its meaning.

pirate	treasures	trade	divers
masts	sailboats	crew	wreck
sailors	cargo		

1. ________________: gold and other riches
2. ________________: goods carried on a ship
3. ________________: people who sail ships
4. ________________: remains of a ruined ship
5. ________________: ships with sails
6. ________________: a group of people who work together on a ship
7. ________________: a kind of ship that carries things people buy
8. ________________: tall wooden poles that hold up sails on ships
9. ________________: a robber of ships at sea
10. ________________: people who work deep in the water

Synonyms

Remember that **synonyms** are words that have the same or almost the same meaning. Circle the two words in each row that are synonyms.

1. poles	masts	boats
2. treasures	riches	movies
3. pages	cargo	goods
4. robber	writer	pirate

Classifying

Study each group of words. Think about how they are alike. Then complete each group with a word from the box.

sailboat	Treasures	Wrecks
crew	Cargo	

1. Boats
____
canoe
rowboat

2. ______________
coins
gold
cups

3. ______________
sugar
salt
flour
tools

4. Groups of People
team
____
class

5. ______________
old building
ruined ship
broken

WORD MAP

Words can be put on a kind of map to show what they have in common. Use the vocabulary words in the box to complete the word map about a ship. Add other words that you know to each group.

pirates	mast	treasures	divers	trade
cargo	crew	sailboat	sailors	

People on a Ship

1. ______________
2. ______________
3. ______________
4. ______________
5. ______________

Parts of a Ship

1. ______________
2. ______________
3. ______________
4. ______________
5. ______________

A SHIP

Things Carried on a Ship

1. ______________
2. ______________
3. ______________
4. ______________
5. ______________

Kinds of Ships

1. ______________
2. ______________
3. ______________
4. ______________
5. ______________

SOCIAL STUDIES
WATER EVERYWHERE
LESSON 13

GET WISE TO TESTS

Directions: Read each sentence. Pick the word that best completes the sentence. Mark the answer space for that word.

Read carefully. Use the other words in the sentences to help you choose each missing word.

1. _____ attacked and robbed the boat.
   Ⓐ Money Ⓑ Pirates Ⓒ Storming Ⓓ Traded

2. They stole gold and other _____.
   Ⓕ mostly Ⓖ sailed Ⓗ day Ⓙ treasures

3. The _____ held the sails up.
   Ⓐ masts Ⓑ sailors Ⓒ driving Ⓓ listen

4. Boats moved by wind are called _____.
   Ⓕ rowed Ⓖ thin Ⓗ sailboats Ⓙ steaming

5. The ship sunk, and later the _____ was found.
   Ⓐ wreck Ⓑ sink Ⓒ searched Ⓓ cooking

6. The ship's _____ worked hard.
   Ⓕ her Ⓖ spell Ⓗ swimming Ⓙ crew

7. The _____ worked underwater.
   Ⓐ swam Ⓑ divers Ⓒ only Ⓓ deep

8. The _____ raised the sails.
   Ⓕ diving Ⓖ sailors Ⓗ treasures Ⓙ dishes

9. Tea and other goods carried on a ship are called _____.
   Ⓐ golden Ⓑ we Ⓒ cargo Ⓓ mast

10. Things to buy are carried on _____ ships.
    Ⓕ quickly Ⓖ hungry Ⓗ trade Ⓙ plate

Writing

The pictures on this page show a sailboat and a canoe. Have you ever been on either kind of boat? Which one would you like to go on?

Write a paragraph telling which boat you chose. Think about the size of the boat. Tell where you might be able to travel and what you might do on your boat. Use some vocabulary words in your writing.

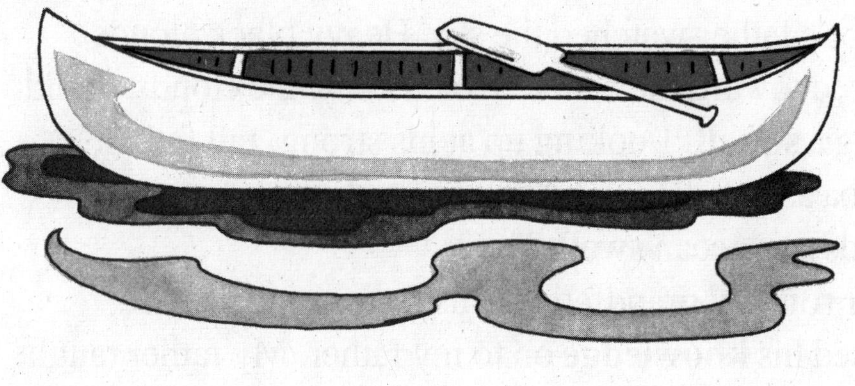

Turn to "My Word List" on page 132. Write some words from the story or other words that you would like to know more about. Use a dictionary to find the meanings.

★ Read the story below. Think about the meanings of the **boldfaced** words. ★

Storm at Sea

In this Hawaiian tale, Koloa sails with his family. His father knows the seas well. But the powerful wind, Ho'olua, brings a storm that tests Koloa.

Koloa's father watched the sky. Heavy black clouds moved toward the canoe. Koloa knew the clouds would bring a **squall**. Looking up at his strong, tall father, Koloa asked, "How did you learn about the stars and winds and ocean **swells**?"

"From my grandfather," his father replied. "He passed his **knowledge** on to my father. My father taught me, and I'm teaching you. You are a good pupil."

Koloa smiled. He wanted to be a **master** navigator when he grew up.

Raindrops began to fall on Koloa's back. Wind whirled about the canoe. Ho'olua, the strong wind, had struck. Swells pounded the sides of the canoe. Rain poured from the sky.

A giant **gust** caught the sails, turning the canoe about. "Lower the sails," Koloa's father commanded.

Winds tried to tear the steering-sweep from Koloa's hands. He knew he must hold the sweep steady. He couldn't ask for help – everyone on the canoe was busy. His mother helped to bring down the masts and sails. Other crew members **bailed** water from the hulls. Koloa alone had to handle the sweep.

Wind roared in his ears. Rain drenched his skin. Huge waves slapped his face. Koloa could hardly see or hear. But he must hold that sweep.

His arms ached. His legs felt like stone. His strength was slipping away. If only he could rest – for just a moment.

Lightning zithered across the sky, followed by roaring thunder. The world was a mass of water, tossing from the sea, tumbling from the sky, whirling in the air. Koloa was wet and cold and hungry. The great wind was pulling the sweep from his arms. Ho'olua was steering the canoe!

But, no! Koloa couldn't let that happen! Ho'olua would turn the canoe over. They might drown in the **raging** sea. Koloa could not let Ho'olua have the canoe. But he was weak. So tired and weak.

His father was speaking to Koloa. Wind roared. Thunder blared. Koloa couldn't hear what his father was saying. But the master navigator's dark eyes flashed **encouragement**.

My father has given me a man's job, Koloa told himself. I must prove that I can handle it.

His legs and arms were tense. His hands gripped the sweep. He no longer heard the wind. He no longer felt the water. He didn't think about his **aching** muscles. He just held tight to that steering-sweep. How long he held it, he didn't know.

Slowly he realized the wind wasn't as strong. Waves no longer poured into the canoe. Soon only a light drizzle of rain tapped the **deck**.

"The storm is ending," his father said. "You did well, my son. You may rest now."

From Storm at Sea, by Nancy Alpert Mower

★ Go back to the story. Underline any words or sentences that give you clues to the meanings of the **boldfaced** words. ★

LITERATURE
WATER EVERYWHERE
LESSON 14

CONTEXT CLUES

Read each sentence. Look for clues to help you complete each sentence with a word from the box. Write the word on the line.

master	swells	knowledge	gust
squall	raging	encouragement	deck
bailed	aching		

1. Facts and _______________ about the sea and the wind can help you sail safely.
2. A _______________ sailor can handle a boat.
3. Sailing in a bad _______________, or storm, can be frightening.
4. The _______________ winds, louder than anyone's voice, can scare you.
5. The huge waves, or _______________, could make the boat turn over.
6. During a bad storm, water may have to be _______________ from the boat.
7. Sometimes a _______________ of wind blows the water right back in.
8. Working on a boat during a storm leaves your body tired and _______________.
9. A person needs _______________ to keep up the hard work on a boat.
10. After a storm, it feels wonderful to stand alone on the _______________ of a boat.

Multiple Meanings

The words in the box have more than one meaning. Look for clues in each sentence to tell which meaning is being used. Write the letter of the meaning next to the correct sentence.

deck	swells
a. floor of a ship	**a.** large waves
b. pack of playing cards	**b.** grows larger

_____ **1.** She mopped the deck until it was shiny.

_____ **2.** The deck had only three queens.

_____ **3.** My finger swells if it is stung by a bee.

_____ **4.** The swells made the boats bob up and down.

Dictionary Skills

Turn to the Dictionary, beginning on page 133. Write each word's meaning next to it.

1. knowledge: ______________________________

2. squall: ______________________________

3. raging: ______________________________

4. bailed: ______________________________

5. gust: ______________________________

6. encouragement: ______________________________

7. aching: ______________________________

8. master: ______________________________

GET WISE TO TESTS

Directions: Read each sentence carefully. Then choose the best answer to complete each sentence. Mark the space for the answer you have chosen.

Tip

This test will show how well you understand the meaning of words. Think about the meaning of the **boldfaced** word before you choose your answer.

1. A **squall** is a kind of _____.
   Ⓐ master Ⓒ storm
   Ⓑ tent Ⓓ prisoner

2. A **raging** storm is frightening and _____.
   Ⓕ loud Ⓗ funny
   Ⓖ slow Ⓙ yellow

3. I **bailed** _____ out of the boat.
   Ⓐ space Ⓒ deck
   Ⓑ water Ⓓ encouragement

4. A **deck** can be a part of a _____.
   Ⓕ gust Ⓗ boat
   Ⓖ car Ⓙ squall

5. A person who has **knowledge** is a person who has _____ something.
   Ⓐ learned Ⓒ baked
   Ⓑ bailed Ⓓ lost

6. When something is **aching**, it _____.
   Ⓕ talks Ⓗ goes
   Ⓖ loops Ⓙ hurts

7. The **swells** in the ocean are _____.
   Ⓐ fish Ⓒ boats
   Ⓑ waves Ⓓ clouds

8. A **master** at something is an _____.
   Ⓕ expert Ⓗ uncle
   Ⓖ ear Ⓙ idea

9. **Encouragement** gives a person _____.
   Ⓐ money Ⓒ swells
   Ⓑ food Ⓓ hope

10. A **gust** is a kind of _____.
    Ⓕ knowledge Ⓗ wind
    Ⓖ deck Ⓙ encouragement

Writing

Koloa had to be very brave to sail during the bad storm. Think about a time when you or someone you know had to be very brave. It may have been during a time of sickness or an accident.

Write a paragraph telling what happened and explain the brave act. Use some vocabulary words in your writing.

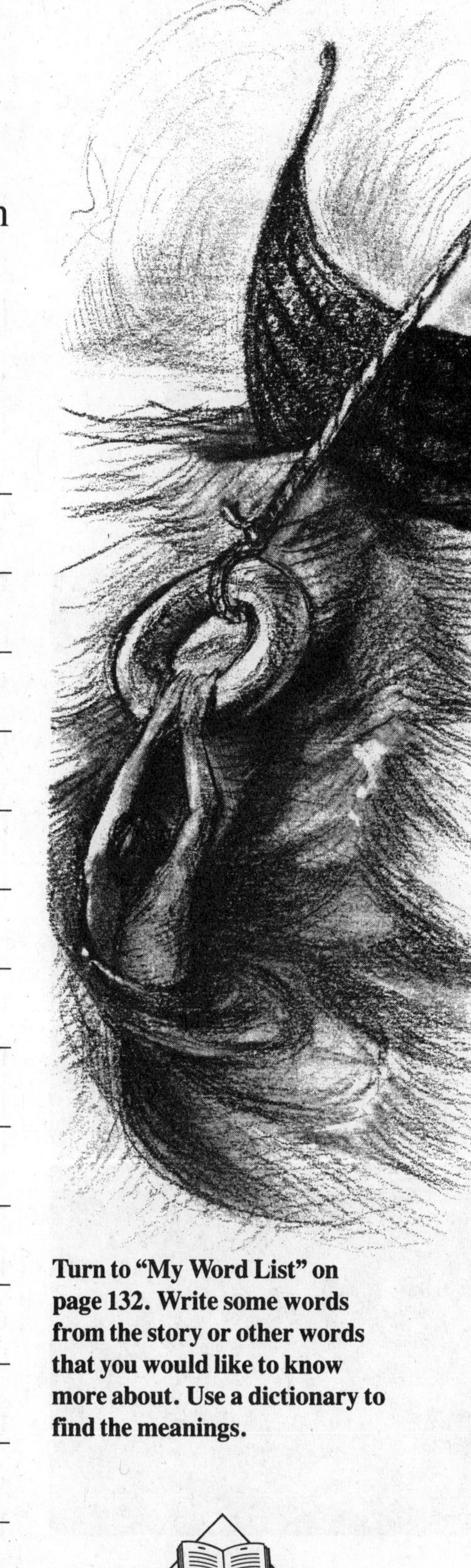

Turn to "My Word List" on page 132. Write some words from the story or other words that you would like to know more about. Use a dictionary to find the meanings.

★ Read the story below. Think about the meanings of the **boldfaced** words. ★

A Whale of a Story

What lives in the ocean, is the largest animal on earth, and is not a fish? The answer is the blue **whale**. The blue whale is a huge **creature**. It can grow up to 100 feet long. It can **weigh** more than 200,000 pounds. That is more than 100 **tons**. A baby blue whale, or **calf**, may weigh as much as two tons at birth. That is a big baby!

All whales belong to a group of animals called **mammals**. Dogs, cats, and horses are mammals. You are a mammal, too. Mammals are different from fish in several ways. Mammals have bigger and better brains than fish do. All mammals give **birth** to live babies, while most fish lay eggs. Also, mammals feed their babies milk. Fish don't. In fact, most fish don't feed their babies at all.

Mammals have lungs. They must get oxygen from the air, so whales have to come up out of the water to breathe. However, whales can hold their breath for a long time. Some can swim **underwater** for over an hour. Then – whoosh – up they come, blowing out used-up air and breathing in fresh air. Fish have gills instead of lungs. They can get oxygen from water. They don't need to come out of the water to breathe.

Blue whales are **massive** creatures. You might think that they eat other large animals. However, their **diet** is mostly very tiny shrimplike animals. It takes a lot of little creatures to feed these giant mammals!

★ Go back to the story. Underline the words or sentences that give you a clue to the meaning of each **boldfaced** word. ★

Context Clues

Read each sentence. Look for clues to help you complete each sentence with a word from the box. Write the word on the line.

whale	mammals	birth	calf
weigh	creature	diet	underwater
tons	massive		

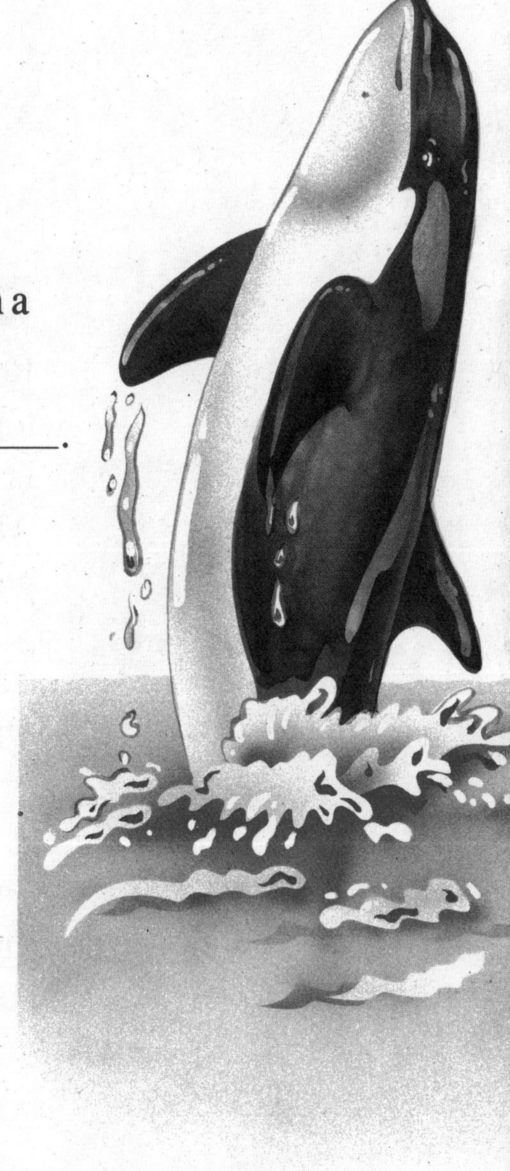

1. A ________________ is a huge sea animal.
2. A baby whale is called a ________________.
3. Whales give ________________ to one baby.
4. Some baby whales ________________ more than a grown elephant.
5. The baby whales may weigh two ________________.
6. Baby whales may seem big, but adult whales are ________________.
7. In fact, the blue whale is the biggest ________________ on earth.
8. It is funny that such big creatures eat a ________________ of small animals.
9. As whales swim ________________, they eat these animals.
10. Whales live in the sea, but they are ________________ just like people.

SCIENCE
WATER EVERYWHERE
LESSON 15

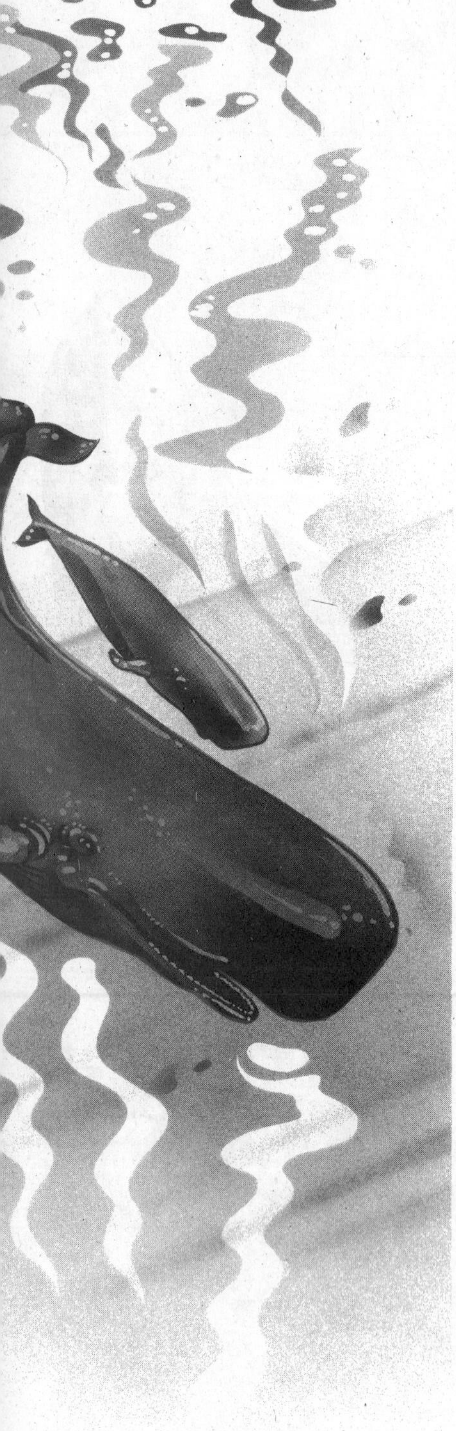

Word Groups

Read each pair of words. Think about how they are alike. Write the word from the box that best completes each word group.

mammals	massive	diet	tons

1. big, huge, ____________________
2. fish, birds, ____________________
3. food, meal, ____________________
4. ounces, pounds, ____________________

Dictionary Skills

Remember that **guide words** are the two words at the top of each dictionary page. They show the first and last words on a page. All the words in between are in ABC order. Decide which words from the box would go on each page. Write the words in ABC order.

whale	underwater	calf	weigh
birth	creature	tons	diet

bell / dog	tent / win
____________________	____________________
____________________	____________________
____________________	____________________
____________________	____________________

GET WISE TO TESTS

Directions: Fill in the space for the word that fits best in the sentence.

Before you choose an answer, try reading the sentence with each answer choice. This will help you choose the answer that makes sense.

1. The largest living animal swims in the ocean. It is a _____.
Ⓐ giraffe Ⓒ whale
Ⓑ snail Ⓓ elephant

2. Whales are quite heavy. They _____ a lot.
Ⓕ drink Ⓗ diet
Ⓖ weigh Ⓙ feel

3. A whale makes many sounds. It is an interesting _____.
Ⓐ noise Ⓒ tons
Ⓑ fish Ⓓ creature

4. A mother whale does not hatch eggs. She gives _____ to a live baby.
Ⓕ birth Ⓗ bath
Ⓖ diet Ⓙ food

5. A blue whale is even bigger than an elephant. It can weigh 100 _____.
Ⓐ creature Ⓒ tons
Ⓑ inches Ⓓ feet

6. A whale needs air to breathe. It can stay _____ for 75 minutes.
Ⓕ on land Ⓗ underwater
Ⓖ cold Ⓙ in the air

7. A whale finds its food in the sea. Its _____ is tiny animals.
Ⓐ trade Ⓒ birth
Ⓑ diet Ⓓ trips

8. Whales do not have four legs and body hair. But they are still _____.
Ⓕ snakes Ⓗ fish
Ⓖ whales Ⓙ mammals

9. Whales are very large. They are _____.
Ⓐ tiny Ⓒ colored
Ⓑ wrinkled Ⓓ massive

10. Even baby whales may weigh a lot. A _____ may weigh two tons.
Ⓕ plant Ⓗ herd
Ⓖ calf Ⓙ bull

Writing

Many people go out on boats for whale watching. Imagine that you are on one of these boats and that you are the first one to see a whale.

Describe what you saw and said during this exciting experience. Use some vocabulary words in your writing.

Suddenly I saw a whale and her calf rise up out of the water! I shouted ______________________________

____

____

____

____

____

____

____

____

____

____

____

____

____

____

Turn to "My Word List" on page 132. Write some words from the story or other words that you would like to know more about. Use a dictionary to find the meanings.

★ Read the story below. Think about the meanings of the **boldfaced** words. ★

Life in the Sea

Deep, deep in the ocean, where the sunlight never reaches, live many strange fish. On the **average**, deep-ocean fish swim about two miles under the water. Some, like the lantern fish, have "lights" on their bodies. Others have **enormous** stomachs and can eat fish twice their size.

Fish in deep water look different from fish that live in shallower water. This is because food is **scarce**, or hard to find, in deep water. Plants cannot grow so far **beneath** the **surface** because sunlight cannot reach there. So nature has helped fish that live at great **depths**. It has given them lights and sharp teeth – the things they need to find and catch other fish to eat.

Near the shore where the water is not so deep, live fish and sea animals that we know better. Here, fish hide in green and brown weeds, turtles swim, and seals play. Below the ocean's surface, you can see many colorful fish that are yellow, blue, and red.

In shallow water, there is **plenty** of food. Many sea plants and tiny water animals live in these sunny **areas**. There is even enough food to feed **mammoth** sea animals, like huge whales.

The **vast** ocean is so large, it can be home to many kinds of fish. As you can see, the fish swimming in our oceans live in very different ways.

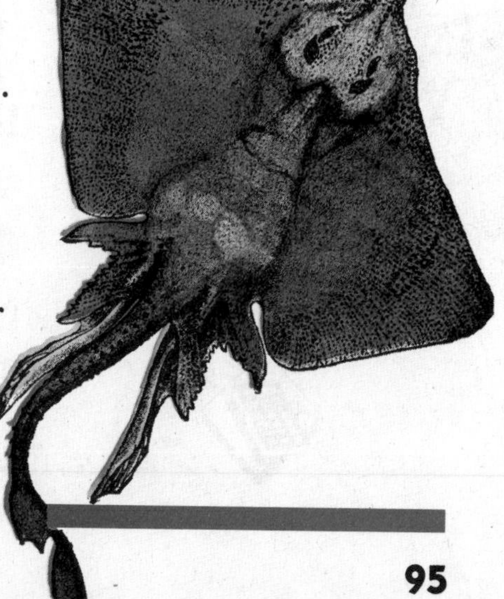

★ Go back to the story. Underline the words or sentences that give you a clue to the meaning of each **boldfaced** word. ★

Using Context

Meanings for the vocabulary words are given below. Go back to the story and read each sentence that has a vocabulary word. If you still cannot tell the meaning, look for clues in the sentences that come before and after the one with the vocabulary word. Write each word in front of its meaning.

beneath	**vast**	**areas**	**plenty**
surface	**depths**	**scarce**	**enormous**
mammoth	**average**		

1. ____________________: deepest part
2. ____________________: the middle or usual amount
3. ____________________: very big
4. ____________________: huge
5. ____________________: places
6. ____________________: difficult to find
7. ____________________: below
8. ____________________: all that is needed
9. ____________________: the top or outer part
10. ____________________: a very great area

CHALLENGE YOURSELF

Name two animals other than whales that are <u>mammoth</u>.

____________________ ____________________

Synonyms

Remember that **synonyms** are words that have the same or almost the same meaning. Match the words in the box with their synonyms listed below. Write each word on the line.

areas	**beneath**	**mammoth**
depth	**average**	

1. huge ______________________
2. deepness ______________________
3. below ______________________
4. places ______________________
5. usual ______________________

Antonyms

Remember that **antonyms** are words that have opposite meanings. Match the words in the box with their antonyms listed below. Write each word on the line.

scarce	**enormous**	**surface**
beneath	**plenty**	

1. enough ______________________
2. few ______________________
3. tiny ______________________
4. bottom ______________________
5. above ______________________

WORD GAME

Write a word from the box next to each clue. Then read the word formed by the boxed letters. The word names an underwater place where some fish live.

surface	average	vast	areas
mammoth	plenty	depths	scarce
beneath	enormous		

1. rare _ ☐ _ _ _ _
2. very great area _ ☐ _ _
3. usual amount _ ☐ _ _ _ _ _
4. deep down in the ocean _ ☐ _ _ _ _
5. the top or outer part _ _ _ _ _ _ _
6. huge _ _ _ _ _ _ _
7. places _ _ _ _ _
8. very big _ _ _ _ _ _ _ _
9. enough, all that is needed _ _ _ _ _ _
10. under; below _ _ _ _ _ _ _

GET WISE TO TESTS

Directions: Find the word or words that mean the same or almost the same as the boldfaced word. Mark your answer.

Think about the meaning of the **boldfaced** word before you choose an answer. Don't be fooled by a word that looks like the **boldfaced** word.

1. **mammoth** animal
   - Ⓐ very small
   - Ⓑ hungry
   - Ⓒ funny
   - Ⓓ huge

2. **beneath** the boat
   - Ⓕ below
   - Ⓖ above
   - Ⓗ near
   - Ⓙ beside

3. dangerous **areas**
   - Ⓐ people
   - Ⓑ animals
   - Ⓒ places
   - Ⓓ waves

4. **scarce** fish
   - Ⓕ common
   - Ⓖ rare
   - Ⓗ scared
   - Ⓙ hungry

5. **vast** ocean
   - Ⓐ fast
   - Ⓑ very small
   - Ⓒ very great
   - Ⓓ best

6. **depths** of the sea
   - Ⓕ deepest part
   - Ⓖ colors
   - Ⓗ islands
   - Ⓙ outer part

7. **plenty** of food
   - Ⓐ kinds
   - Ⓑ names
   - Ⓒ types
   - Ⓓ enough

8. **average** amount
   - Ⓕ strange
   - Ⓖ added
   - Ⓗ awful
   - Ⓙ usual

9. **enormous** mouth
   - Ⓐ very big
   - Ⓑ very tiny
   - Ⓒ very ugly
   - Ⓓ hanging open

10. water's **surface**
    - Ⓕ bottom
    - Ⓖ top
    - Ⓗ floor
    - Ⓙ middle

Review

1. whale's **calf**
   - Ⓐ cow
   - Ⓑ baby
   - Ⓒ father
   - Ⓓ cat

2. regular **diet**
   - Ⓕ desk
   - Ⓖ group
   - Ⓗ food
   - Ⓙ home

Imagine that you are in a special ship that takes you down to the ocean floor. You are writing in a notebook about your experiences.

Finish the notebook page below by telling what you see. Use the picture and what you have read for ideas. Use some vocabulary words in your writing.

Today I took an exciting trip down to the ocean floor.

The first thing I saw was ______________________

____

____

____

____

____

____

____

____

____

____

____

Turn to "My Word List" on page 132. Write some words from the story or other words that you would like to know more about. Use a dictionary to find the meanings.

★ To review the words in Lessons 13–16, turn to page 128. ★

MAKING MUSIC

Music is the art of mixing sounds, usually with instruments or voices. Music can change our moods. It can make us feel happy or sad, thoughtful or relaxed.

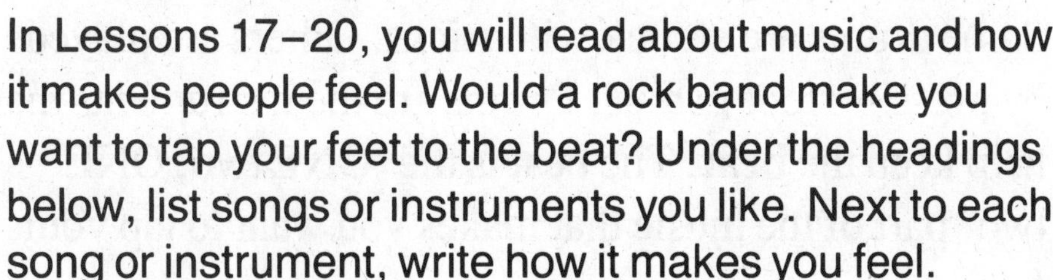

In Lessons 17–20, you will read about music and how it makes people feel. Would a rock band make you want to tap your feet to the beat? Under the headings below, list songs or instruments you like. Next to each song or instrument, write how it makes you feel.

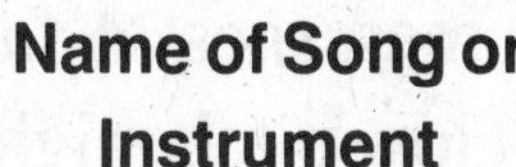

Name of Song or Instrument	How It Makes Me Feel

★ Read the story below. Think about the meanings of the **boldfaced** words. ★

There Is Music in the Air

What is music? Music is sound. Sound is made when a material moves back and forth rapidly. Carefully stretch a rubber band between two rulers. Ask someone to snap one side of it. This will **cause** the rubber band to move quickly. It will make a sound.

A guitar is an **instrument** that makes music. If you stretch a guitar string and pluck it, the string will move rapidly and make a soft sound. If you attach the string to a guitar, you'll get a lot more **volume**. Why is the sound louder now? You are moving the string, the wood of the guitar, and the air inside it. If you stretch the string to **tighten** it, you will get a higher sound, like "ping." This is called a high **pitch**. If you loosen the string, the pitch will sound lower, like "pong."

A drum is another **musical** instrument. Its sound is made by tapping on a stretched piece of plastic or hide. Some drums are **struck** with sticks. Others are played by pressing foot **pedals**. Drums are the instruments that help keep the **beat**. The beat is the "ONE two, ONE two" part of the music that makes you want to tap your feet.

Music can **communicate** many messages. A fast beat might make you feel happy. A low pitch might make you feel sad. Whatever instrument is used, music has something to say.

★ Go back to the story. Underline the words or sentences that give you a clue to the meaning of each **boldfaced** word. ★

Using Context

Meanings for the vocabulary words are given below. Go back to the story and read each sentence that has a vocabulary word. If you still cannot tell the meaning, look for clues in the sentences that come before and after the one with the vocabulary word. Write each word in front of its meaning.

cause	volume	tighten	pitch
pedals	instrument	musical	struck
beat	communicate		

1. ____________________: having to do with music

2. ____________________: to receive and send messages

3. ____________________: a reason something happens

4. ____________________: bars pressed down by the foot

5. ____________________: something used to make music

6. ____________________: how high or low a sound is

7. ____________________: to make tight

8. ____________________: how loud a sound is

9. ____________________: the part of music you tap your feet to

10. ____________________: hit

SCIENCE
MAKING MUSIC
LESSON 17

Word Groups

Read each pair of words. Think about how they are alike. Write the word from the box that best completes each word group.

cause	communicate	volume	struck

1. louder, noisier, ______________________
2. slapped, plucked, ____________________
3. reason, purpose, _____________________
4. sing, talk, __________________________

Cloze Paragraph

Use the words in the box to complete the paragraph. Reread the paragraph to be sure it makes sense.

pitch	musical	instrument	beat
tighten	pedals		

A tambourine is my favorite (1) ________________. It has no strings to (2) ________________. It has no (3) ________________ to place my feet on. I do not worry that the (4) ________________ is too high or too low. I just use my hand to tap the (5) ________________ of any song I hear. Someday I will play one in a (6) ________________ show.

WORD MAP

Words can be put on a kind of map to show what they have in common. Write each word from the box in the group where it belongs to tell about musical instruments.

pedals	volume	musical	tighten
pitch	struck	communicate	

Some Parts
keys
strings
____

How Played
plucked
drawing bow
____

INSTRUMENTS

Sound
tone
____
____

Care
clean
polish
____

Reason Played
own pleasure
________________ ideas
________________ entertainment

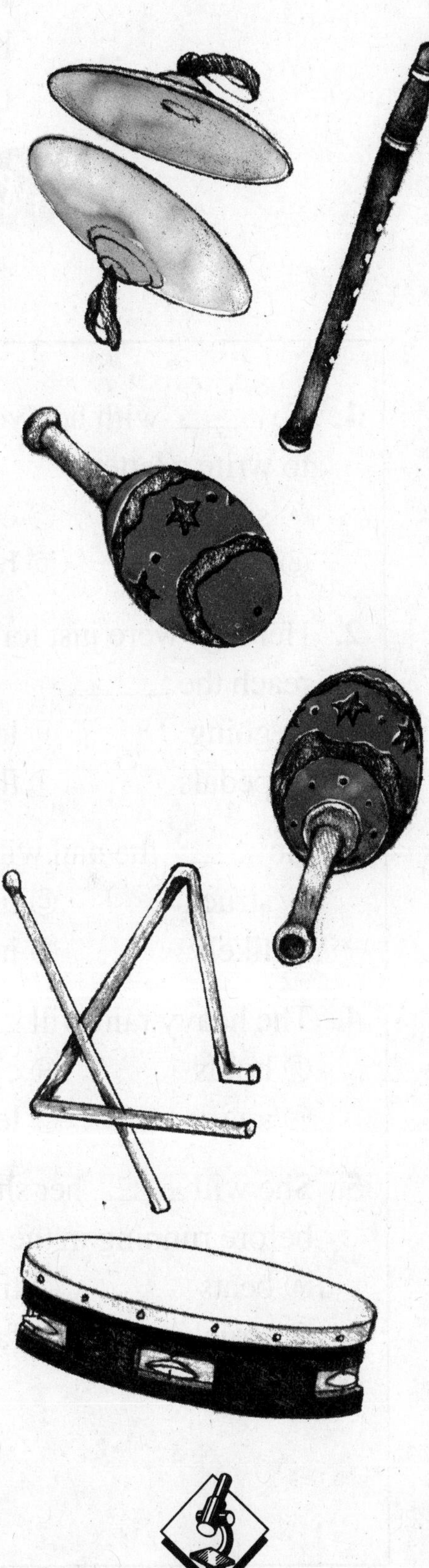

GET WISE TO TESTS

Directions: Read each sentence. Pick the word that best completes the sentence. Mark the answer space for that word.

Before you choose an answer, try reading the sentence with each answer choice. This will help you choose an answer that makes sense.

1. To _____ with her, you will have to write a letter.

Ⓐ sad Ⓒ communicate
Ⓑ crying Ⓓ baker

2. Her legs were just long enough to reach the _____.

Ⓕ going Ⓗ loud
Ⓖ pedals Ⓙ them

3. He _____ the nail with a hammer.

Ⓐ struck Ⓒ tightened
Ⓑ likely Ⓓ jump

4. The heavy rain will _____ a flood.

Ⓕ holds Ⓗ cause
Ⓖ angry Ⓙ lesson

5. She will _____ her shoelaces before running in the race.

Ⓐ beats Ⓒ tighten
Ⓑ struck Ⓓ faked

6. The high _____ of the flute sounds bright and clear.

Ⓕ pedals Ⓗ lots
Ⓖ pitch Ⓙ shelf

7. The _____ was so low I could not hear it.

Ⓐ their Ⓒ volume
Ⓑ lovely Ⓓ sailing

8. We marched to a song with a steady _____.

Ⓕ seated Ⓗ causes
Ⓖ beat Ⓙ watered

9. I want to hear the drums at the _____ show.

Ⓐ musical Ⓒ silent
Ⓑ city Ⓓ laughing

10. The drummer was happy to find her lost _____.

Ⓕ placed Ⓗ instrument
Ⓖ danced Ⓙ volume

Writing

Look at the pictures on this page. Each picture shows an instrument made with things that can be found at home. Think about which instrument you would like to play.

Describe an instrument on this page, or one you think could be made from things at home. Tell what it is made of and how it sounds. Explain how you would create music with it. You may also want to describe the kind of music you would like to play on this instrument. Use some vocabulary words in your writing.

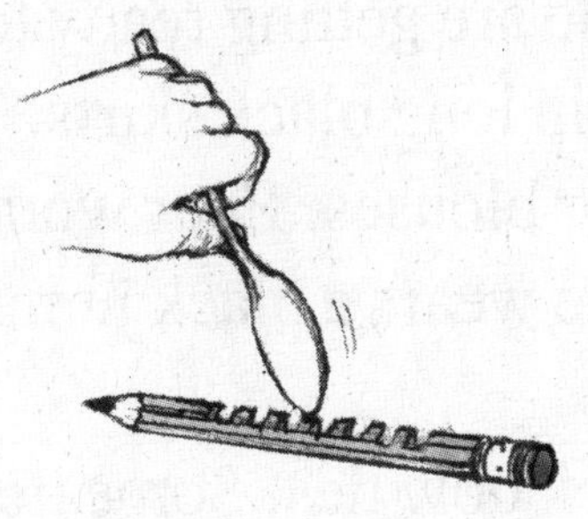

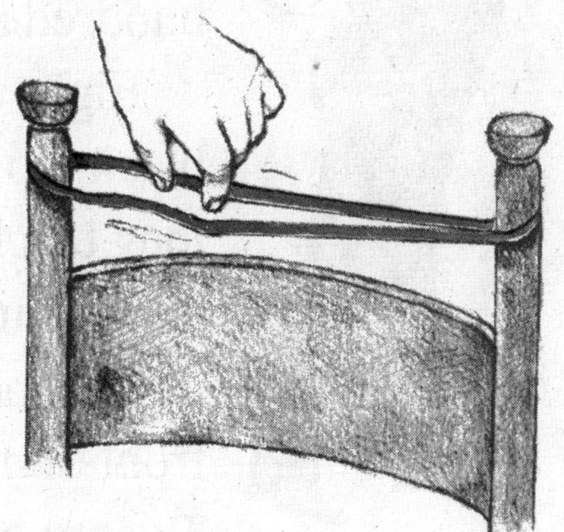

The instrument I would like to play is made of ______

____

____

____

____

____

____

____

____

Turn to "My Word List" on page 132. Write some words from the story or other words that you would like to know more about. Use a dictionary to find the meanings.

★ Read the story below. Think about the meanings of the **boldfaced** words. ★

The Philharmonic Gets Dressed

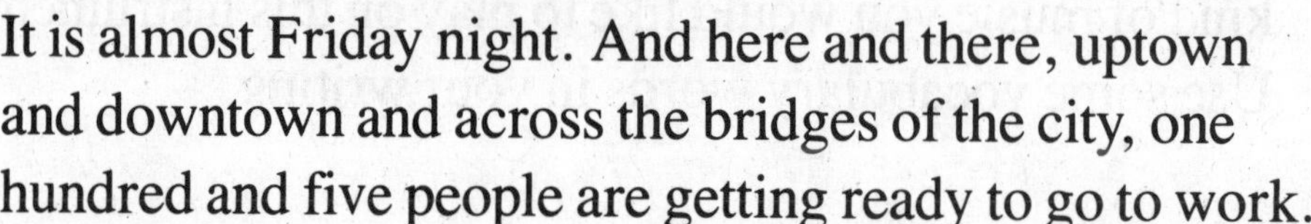

Where are these one hundred and five people going? Why are they all wearing black and white?

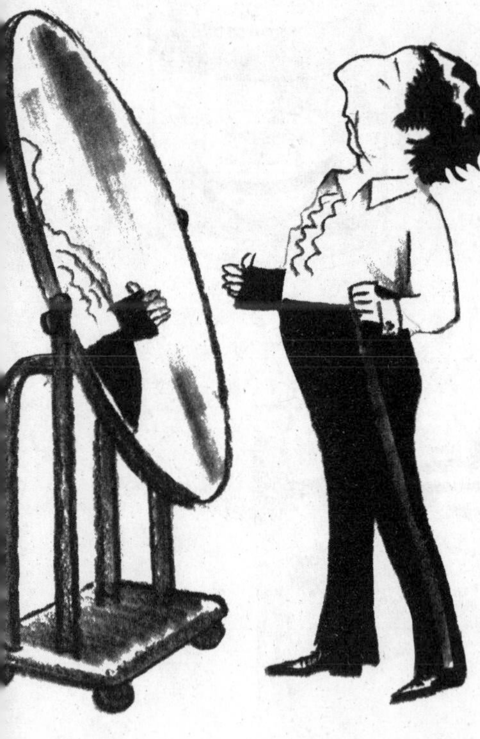

It is almost Friday night. And here and there, uptown and downtown and across the bridges of the city, one hundred and five people are getting ready to go to work.

Eight women dress in long black skirts. They wear black tops, sweaters, or blouses. Four women put on long black dresses. One wears a black jumper over a black shirt.

The men put on black bow ties. Some tie them on in front of **mirrors**. Some stare into space and tie them. Twenty-seven men clip on ties that are already made into bows. A man with wavy black and white hair, a ruffly shirt, and a **cummerbund** ties on a *very* big white bow tie. It looks like a white bat. He slips on a white vest and then a black jacket that is short in the front and long in the back, where it divides in two, like black **beetle** wings. The jacket and pants are called tails. Tonight all the other ninety-one men put on **tuxedo** jackets. These are black, too, with shiny satin lapels.

When all the men and women are completely dressed in black and white, they get ready to go out. They put on overcoats, jackets or capes, boots or rubbers, mittens or gloves, some scarves, many hats, a few earmuffs. Then almost everyone picks up a case.

The man with the dark wavy hair with the white lightning in it, the ruffly shirt, cummerbund, and bow tie that looks like a white bat picks up a very thin leather **briefcase**.

At 8:25 on Friday night in the middle of the city, one hundred and four people walk onto the big stage in Philharmonic Hall.

One hundred and one of them are carrying the musical instruments that were in those cases.

Three people do not carry instruments. Their instruments are too heavy to carry around. They are already on the stage.

There are one hundred and two chairs on the stage, and two **stools**. Near each of these there is a music stand with sheets of music on it. The one hundred and four people take their seats. The double bass players sit on the stools. Everyone turns to the first page of music. It is a white page covered with black lines and musical notes.

The **conductor** raises his **baton** in the air. He brings it down, and the hall, which is as wide and long as a red velvet football field, fills with music.

The music floats and rises.

It is 8:30 on Friday night, and the one hundred and five men and women dressed completely in black and white have gone to work turning the black notes on white pages into a **symphony**.

They are the members of the Philharmonic **Orchestra**, and their work is to play. Beautifully.

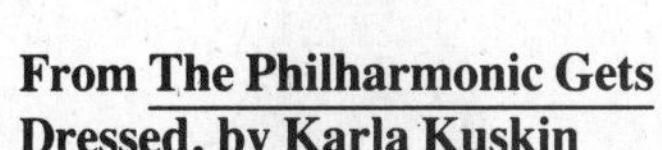

From The Philharmonic Gets Dressed, by Karla Kuskin

★ Go back to the story. Underline any words or sentences that give you clues to the meanings of the **boldfaced** words. ★

LITERATURE
MAKING MUSIC
LESSON 18

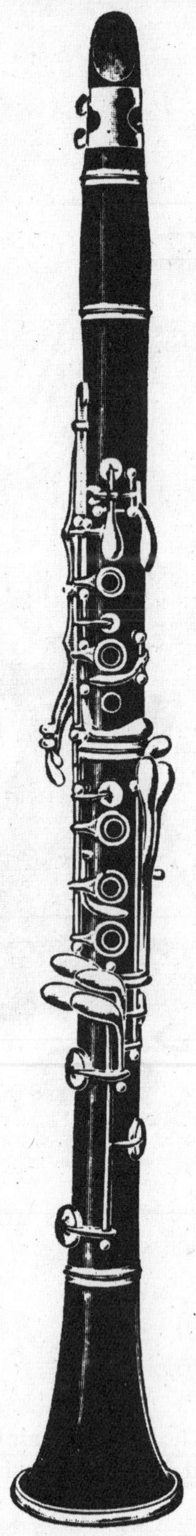

CONTEXT CLUES

Read each sentence. Look for clues to help you complete each sentence with a word from the box. Write the word on the line.

mirrors	symphony	beetle	stools
briefcase	cummerbund	baton	tuxedo
conductor	orchestra		

1. The musicians in the ________________ got ready to play.
2. The men put on ________________ jackets.
3. Each man wore a ________________ around his waist that looked better than a plain belt.
4. They looked at themselves in ________________ as they put on their black bow ties.
5. That man looks like a ________________ in this black jacket!
6. Now the musician takes sheets of music out of his ________________.
7. Some musicians sit on ________________ while they play.
8. The ________________ is ready to lead the orchestra.
9. He raises his ________________, or wand, to start the music.
10. The music in a ________________ is created when many different instruments are played together.

Word Sense

Read each phrase. Check the Dictionary to see if the words make sense together. If they do, write yes on the line. If they do not, write a new word that does make sense with the underlined word.

1. jelly briefcase ______________________
2. dog's cummerbund ______________________
3. folding stools ______________________
4. popcorn beetle ______________________
5. broken mirrors ______________________
6. tuxedo wings ______________________
7. orchestra drives ______________________

Music Words

The words in the box all have to do with music. Write each word beside its meaning.

conductor	symphony	orchestra	baton

1. group of musicians ______________
2. a stick or wand used to direct the playing of music ______________
3. a person who leads musicians ______________
4. a piece of music created when many different instruments are played together ______________

GET WISE TO TESTS

Directions: Read each sentence. Pick the word that best completes the sentence. Mark the answer space for that word.

If you are not sure which word completes the sentence, do the best you can. Try to choose the answer that makes the most sense.

1. Ronald sewed three buttons onto his _____.
   Ⓐ symphony Ⓒ tuxedo
   Ⓑ most Ⓓ repeats

2. Louise made a _____ from black cloth.
   Ⓕ sing Ⓗ her
   Ⓖ conductor Ⓙ cummerbund

3. The store was filled with _____ so people could see themselves.
   Ⓐ mirrors Ⓒ pretty
   Ⓑ throw Ⓓ stools

4. The _____ stands in front of the musicians.
   Ⓕ aiming Ⓗ briefcase
   Ⓖ conductor Ⓙ carried

5. Did you ever hear that _____ before?
   Ⓐ so Ⓒ speaks
   Ⓑ complete Ⓓ symphony

6. The music began when the _____ was raised.
   Ⓕ beetle Ⓗ baton
   Ⓖ sleepy Ⓙ beautifully

7. The piano players sat on round _____.
   Ⓐ stools Ⓒ moving
   Ⓑ they Ⓓ mirrors

8. Please take the papers out of your _____.
   Ⓕ briefcase Ⓗ deep
   Ⓖ thought Ⓙ orchestra

9. The _____ has many musicians.
   Ⓐ baton Ⓒ like
   Ⓑ orchestra Ⓓ speech

10. A _____ sat under a tulip.
   Ⓕ beetle Ⓗ tuxedo
   Ⓖ through Ⓙ sad

Orchestras play many kinds of music. What kind of music do you like to hear most of all? Is it soft and peaceful? Is it loud with lots of drums? Do you enjoy country music the most?

Write a paragraph about your favorite kind of music. Tell why you like it best. If you have two favorite kinds of music, tell about both of them. Use some vocabulary words in your writing.

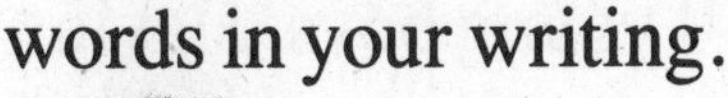

Turn to "My Word List" on page 132. Write some words from the story or other words that you would like to know more about. Use a dictionary to find the meanings.

★ Read the story below. Think about the meanings of the **boldfaced** words. ★

The Boys Choir of Harlem

What makes a group of boys from the streets of Harlem want to give their best day after day? For one group, it is singing together in a special **choir**. The Boys Choir of Harlem is made up of 35 to 40 young boys. Having the chance to be a **singer** in the Boys Choir is exciting.

The boys sing many songs in their two-hour **concerts**. Many of the **melodies** of the songs are familiar to the audience. The choir sings popular tunes of today. They also sing songs written long ago by well-loved **composers** such as J. S. Bach. Members of the choir also **dance** and act. These young boys give **dazzling** shows that amaze the audience.

The choir was founded in 1968 by Dr. Walter Turnbull, a teacher and singer. They began as a church choir in Harlem in New York City. Since then, they have become very **famous**. They have performed at the White House and in many places in Asia and Europe. The choir sang on the soundtrack of the movie Glory, and they have even recorded an album.

Hard work, talent, and the efforts of Dr. Turnbull have helped make the Boys Choir of Harlem a **successful** group. The boys have done well in front of the television **camera** that records their singing and dancing. They have done well in the recording studio and on stage. The boys are also good students. Many say that they have succeeded because of the Boys Choir of Harlem.

★ Go back to the story. Underline the words or sentences that give you a clue to the meaning of each **boldfaced** word. ★

USING CONTEXT

Meanings for the vocabulary words are given below. Go back to the story and read each sentence that has a vocabulary word. If you still cannot tell the meaning, look for clues in the sentences that come before and after the one with the vocabulary word. Write each word in front of its meaning.

dazzling	**choir**	**famous**	**camera**
concerts	**dance**	**successful**	**composers**
melodies	**singer**		

1. ____________________: to move in time to music
2. ____________________: a person who sings
3. ____________________: a group of people who sing together
4. ____________________: tunes
5. ____________________: people who write music
6. ____________________: a machine used to make photographs or movies
7. ____________________: musical shows
8. ____________________: amazing; exciting
9. ____________________: having reached a goal
10. ____________________: well known

FINE ARTS
MAKING MUSIC
LESSON 19

Word Groups

Read each pair of words. Think about how the words are alike. Write the word from the box that best completes each word group.

dazzling	composers	dance
famous	melodies	

1. songs, tunes, ______________________
2. well known, great, ______________________
3. amazing, bright, ______________________
4. writers, creators, ______________________
5. sing, act, ______________________

Cloze Paragraph

Use the words in the box to complete the paragraph. Reread the paragraph to be sure it makes sense.

successful	singer	concerts
melodies	dance	

It would be fun to be a (1) ______________ in a choir. I could learn many new (2) ______________ to sing. In the spring, our choir could give outdoor (3) ______________ at the park. Some of us might even (4) ______________ to the music we sing. If we worked hard to reach our goals, I know we would be (5) ______________.

GET WISE TO TESTS

Directions: Read each sentence carefully. Then choose the best answer to complete each sentence. Mark the space for the answer you have chosen.

Before you choose an answer, try reading the sentence with each answer choice. This will help you choose the answer that makes sense.

1. A **camera** takes _____.
   Ⓐ music Ⓑ photos Ⓒ dishes Ⓓ maps

2. A **singer** often performs on a _____.
   Ⓕ stage Ⓖ table Ⓗ house Ⓙ cloud

3. Everyone in a **choir** has a chance to _____.
   Ⓐ swim Ⓑ write Ⓒ sing Ⓓ kick

4. People who are **famous** are _____.
   Ⓕ well-known Ⓖ noisy Ⓗ hungry Ⓙ unknown

5. **Melodies** can be pleasant to _____.
   Ⓐ touch Ⓑ taste Ⓒ hear Ⓓ see

6. A **successful** person has done _____.
   Ⓕ poorly Ⓖ nothing Ⓗ well Ⓙ badly

7. A **dazzling** dancer is one who is _____.
   Ⓐ sick Ⓑ funny Ⓒ happy Ⓓ splendid

8. The main thing you will hear at **concerts** is _____.
   Ⓕ thunder Ⓖ silence Ⓗ rumbling Ⓙ music

9. Someone who can **dance** well might do some fancy _____.
   Ⓐ pictures Ⓑ steps Ⓒ lessons Ⓓ sounds

10. **Composers** create _____.
    Ⓕ messes Ⓖ gardens Ⓗ jobs Ⓙ songs

FINE ARTS
MAKING MUSIC
LESSON 19

Imagine that you are going to meet the members of the Boys Choir of Harlem. You may write about them for your local newspaper. What would you and your readers like to know about the boys and the choir?

Write at least five questions that you might ask them. Use some vocabulary words in your writing.

1. What do you like best about ______________________

____

2. ____

____

____

3. ____

____

____

4. ____

____

____

5. ____

____

____

Turn to "My Word List" on page 132. Write some words from the story or other words that you would like to know more about. Use a dictionary to find the meanings.

★ Read the story below. Think about the meanings of the **boldfaced** words. ★

Special Times for Music

A feast or party is always a time to **celebrate** with music, song, and dance. At a Native American **festival** you would hear drums, flutes, and rattles. You would also see dances and hear **chants**, the singing of words over and over in a certain pattern.

A Native American **ceremony** also includes music, song, and dance. This special event may be serious, but that doesn't mean that a ceremony is quiet.

Long ago, Native Americans began using music, song, and dance to tell about their daily lives and beliefs. Each **tribe**, or group, held ceremonies and festivals to help it at important times. There were songs and dances to help sick people get well. There were songs and dances of **death** when a person died. There were special dances for hunters to help them catch food, like the Buffalo Dance. Farming tribes held planting ceremonies and **harvest** festivals when the crops were picked. In between, they might do rain and sun dances to help the crops grow.

In many tribes the **elders** taught the younger people these songs and dances. **Grandparents** taught their children's children. These grandchildren became teachers, too. In this way, Native Americans kept the ways of their **ancestors** alive.

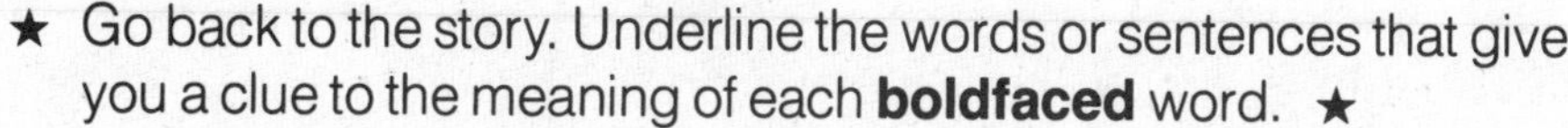

★ Go back to the story. Underline the words or sentences that give you a clue to the meaning of each **boldfaced** word. ★

USING CONTEXT

Meanings for the vocabulary words are given below. Go back to the story and read each sentence that has a vocabulary word. If you still cannot tell the meaning, look for clues in the sentences that come before and after the one with the vocabulary word. Write each word in front of its meaning.

chants	**festival**	**tribe**	**ancestors**
elders	**celebrate**	**death**	**grandparents**
ceremony	**harvest**		

1. ____________________: a feast; a big party

2. ____________________: a serious, special event

3. ____________________: songs with words repeated in almost the same tone of voice

4. ____________________: when crops are gathered

5. ____________________: to honor something with special activities

6. ____________________: older people

7. ____________________: group of people living together

8. ____________________: end of life

9. ____________________: family members who lived long ago

10. ____________________: the parents of parents

Word Groups

Read each group of words. Think about how they are alike. Write the word from the box that best completes each word group.

festival	celebrate	grandparent	death

1. mother, father, aunt, ______________________

2. party, fair, feast, ______________________

3. perform, enjoy, honor, ______________________

4. end, stop, finish, ______________________

Dictionary Skills

Read each question. For a "yes" answer, write the word yes on the line. For a "no" answer, write a sentence that gives the correct meaning of the underlined word. Use the Dictionary if you need help.

1. Is an ancestor someone who has not been born?

____

2. Is a harvest the time when crops are picked?

____

3. Are chants things you can touch with your hands?

____

4. Is a tribe made up of people who know each other?

____

SOCIAL STUDIES
MAKING MUSIC
LESSON 20

HIDDEN MESSAGE PUZZLE

Write a word from the box next to each clue. To find the message, copy the numbered letters in the matching numbered boxes at the bottom of the page. Then you will know other special times for music.

ancestor	celebrate	death	elders
festival	ceremony	tribe	chant

1. kind of song ☐☐☐☐☐ (box 3 = 6)
2. family member who lived long ago ☐☐☐☐☐☐☐☐ (box 7 = 2)
3. opposite of birth ☐☐☐☐☐ (box 5 = 1)
4. feast ☐☐☐☐☐☐☐☐ (box 3 = 8)
5. older people ☐☐☐☐☐☐ (box 3 = 5)
6. special event ☐☐☐☐☐☐☐☐ (box 8 = 7)
7. a group of people who live together ☐☐☐☐☐ (box 3 = 4)
8. to honor ☐☐☐☐☐☐☐☐☐ (box 3 = 3)

ANSWER: ☐☐☐☐☐☐☐☐
1 2 3 4 5 6 7 8

GET WISE TO TESTS

Directions: Read the phrase. Look for the word or words that have the same or almost the same meaning as the boldfaced word. Mark the letter for your choice.

Always read all the answer choices. Many choices may make sense. But only one answer choice has the same or almost the same meaning as the **boldfaced** word.

1. loud **chants**
   Ⓐ sports Ⓒ songs
   Ⓑ events Ⓓ charts

2. good **harvest**
   Ⓕ seeds planted Ⓗ machines
   Ⓖ crops picked Ⓙ hairs

3. happy **festival**
   Ⓐ party Ⓒ studio
   Ⓑ tent Ⓓ farm

4. let us **celebrate**
   Ⓕ study Ⓗ honor
   Ⓖ sleep Ⓙ announce

5. ancient **ancestors**
   Ⓐ dreams Ⓒ farm helpers
   Ⓑ animals Ⓓ family members

6. his **grandparents**
   Ⓕ pals Ⓗ actors
   Ⓖ teachers Ⓙ parents' parents

7. group's **elders**
   Ⓐ children Ⓒ classmates
   Ⓑ older people Ⓓ pets

8. person's **death**
   Ⓕ end Ⓗ place
   Ⓖ birth Ⓙ home

9. wedding **ceremony**
   Ⓐ story Ⓒ painting
   Ⓑ serious event Ⓓ puppets

10. Native American **tribe**
    Ⓕ pride Ⓗ group of people
    Ⓖ language Ⓙ nest of birds

Review

1. good **concerts**
   Ⓐ musical shows Ⓒ games
   Ⓑ zoos Ⓓ stories

2. **dazzling** act
   Ⓕ dangerous Ⓗ terrible
   Ⓖ splendid Ⓙ sad

You have just learned some ways that Native Americans celebrate. Think about some events that you and your family celebrate.

Write a letter to a friend about something that you celebrate. You may want to invite your friend to join the celebration. Be sure you describe why and how you celebrate. Use some vocabulary words in your writing.

____
(Date)

Dear ____________________,

Sincerely,

____

Turn to "My Word List" on page 132. Write some words from the story or other words that you would like to know more about. Use a dictionary to find the meanings.

★ To review the words in Lessons 17–20, turn to page 129. ★

REVIEW

Read each clue. Then write the word from the box that fits the clue. Use the Dictionary if you need help.

extinct	increase	height	lumber
terrifying	continent	moist	approached

1. When you pedal a bike faster, you do this to its speed. ________________
2. When you measure how tall you are, you find this. ________________
3. If there are no more of an animal, it is this. ________________
4. People make this when they cut trees into boards. ________________
5. This is a large area of land, such as South America. ________________
6. This is what you did to your home if you walked toward it. ________________
7. You can use this word to describe very scary things. ________________
8. This is how the ground will be after a rain. ________________

REVIEW

Read each question. Think about the meaning of the underlined word. Then write yes or no to answer the question. Use the Dictionary if you need help.

1. Can hard work be exhausting? ________
2. Would you find canvas on your plate at dinner? ________
3. Is it dangerous to wear a helmet if you ride a skateboard? ________
4. Could a professional dancer make money by dancing? ________
5. Does a clown entertain people? ________
6. Would you find confidence in the bottom of your closet? ________
7. Should you respond to someone when you are asked a question? ________
8. If you want glossy hair, do you want it to be curly? ________
9. Could an actor wear a costume in a play? ________
10. If you outgrow your shoes, do they still fit well? ________

REVIEW

Read each clue. Then write the word from the box that fits the clue. Use the Dictionary if you need help.

sparkled	**talent**	**arrange**	**orchard**
refuse	**television**	**enchanted**	**imaginary**

1. If you are pleased very much by this story, you might be this. ________________

2. If you are a great artist, people say you have this. ________________

3. You can go to this kind of place to pick apples or peaches. ________________

4. This is what you can turn on to watch a football game. ________________

5. When you put a group of words in ABC order, you do this to them. ________________

6. If you say no, you do this. ________________

7. If a diamond shone brightly, this is what it did. ________________

8. The characters in cartoons are this. ________________

REVIEW

Read each question. Think about the meaning of the underlined word. Then use yes or no to answer the question. Use the Dictionary if you need help.

1. If you bailed water from a boat, did you drink it? ________
2. Can you weigh yourself with a ruler? ________
3. Is it possible to talk to the crew of a ship? ________
4. If you have an aching tooth, should you see a dentist? ________
5. If food is scarce, does everyone have too much to eat? ________
6. Could divers probably help you look for sunken treasure? ________
7. Should you trust a pirate with your ship? ________
8. Will a massive creature fit in a pocket? ________
9. Can a person walk around a vast city in ten minutes? ________
10. If a squall is coming, should you probably go to a safe place? ________

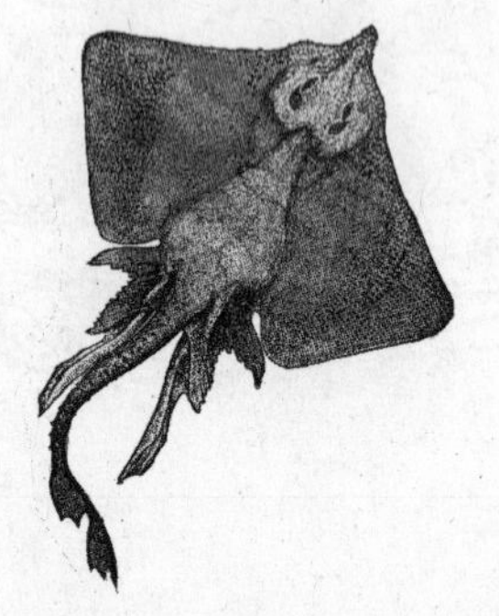

REVIEW

Read each clue. Then write the word from the box that fits the clue. Use the Dictionary if you need help.

struck	baton	tuxedo	communicate
famous	celebrate	dazzling	ancestors

1. You might be this if millions of people know who you are. ________________
2. If you conduct a band, you might wave and tap this. ________________
3. When you do something special on your birthday, you do this. ________________
4. If you hit a drum, you did this to it. ________________
5. A man who wants to dress up in evening clothes would wear this. ________________
6. This is what two people do when they talk to each other. ________________
7. You might use this word to tell about an amazing performer. ________________
8. These are family members from long ago. ________________

REVIEW AND WRITE

In this book, you have read about many people and the work they do. Some people you have read about explored the jungle. Some worked in the circus. Others tell stories, find buried treasure, and make music. What kind of work would you like to do? Write about a job you would like to have. Tell why you want to do that kind of work. Use some of the vocabulary words you have learned.

My Word List

This is your word list. Here you can write words from the stories. You can also write other words that you would like to know more about. Use a dictionary to find the meaning of each word. Then write the meaning next to the word.

UNIT 1
JUNGLES AND TROPICS

UNIT 2
IN THE SPOTLIGHT

My Word List

UNIT 3
IMAGINARY CHARACTERS

UNIT 4
WATER EVERYWHERE

UNIT 5
MAKING MUSIC

DICTIONARY

ENTRY

Each word in a dictionary is called an **entry word**. Study the parts of an entry in the sample shown below. Think about how each part will help you when you read and write.

① **Entry Word** An entry word is boldfaced. A dot is used to divide the word into syllables.

② **Pronunciation** This special spelling shows you how to say the word. Look at the pronunciation key below. It tells you the symbols that stand for sounds.

③ **Part of Speech** The abbreviation tells you the part of speech. In this entry *v.* stands for verb.

④ **Words with Spelling Changes** When the spelling of a word changes after *-ed* or *-ing* is added, the spelling is shown in an entry.

⑤ **Definition** A definition is given for each entry word. The definition tells what the word means.

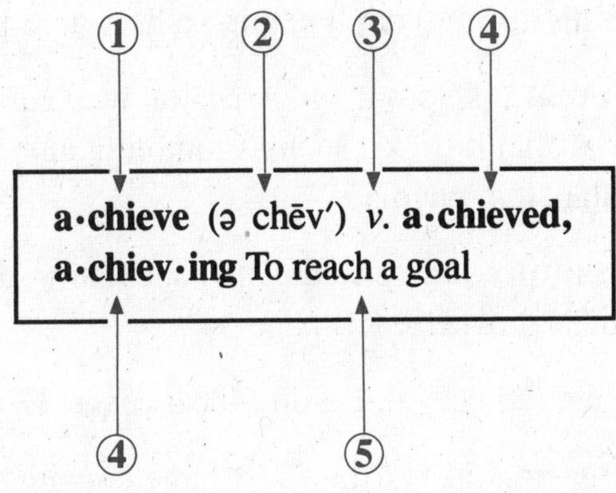

PRONUNCIATION KEY

A **pronunciation key** is a helpful tool. It shows you the symbols, or special signs, for the sounds in English. Next to each symbol is a sample word for that sound. Use the key to help you with the pronunciation given after each entry word.

a	at, **bad**
ā	ape, **pain**, **day**, **break**
ä	father, **car**, **heart**
âr	care, **pair**, **bear**, **their**, **where**
e	end, **pet**, **said**, **heaven**, **friend**
ē	equal, **me**, **feet**, **team**, **piece**, **key**
i	it, **big**, **English**, **hymn**
ī	ice, **fine**, **lie**, **my**
îr	ear, **deer**, **here**, **pierce**
o	odd, **hot**, **watch**
ō	old, **oat**, **toe**, **low**
ô	coffee, **all**, **taught**, **law**, **fought**
ôr	order, **fork**, **horse**, **story**, **pour**
oi	oil, **toy**
ou	out, **now**
u	up, **mud**, **love**, **double**
ū	use, **mule**, **cue**, **feud**, **few**
ü	rule, **true**, **food**
u̇	put, **wood**, **should**
ûr	burn, **hurry**, **term**, **bird**, **word**, **courage**
ə	about, **taken**, **pencil**, **lemon**, **circus**
b	bat, **above**, **job**
ch	chin, **such**, **match**
d	dear, **soda**, **bad**
f	five, **defend**, **leaf**, **off**, **cough**, **elephant**
g	game, **ago**, **fog**, **egg**
h	hat, **ahead**
hw	white, **whether**, **which**
j	joke, **enjoy**, **gem**, **page**, **edge**
k	kite, **bakery**, **seek**, **tack**, **cat**
l	lid, **sailor**, **feel**, **ball**, **allow**
m	man, **family**, **dream**
n	not, **final**, **pan**, **knife**
ng	long, **singer**, **pink**
p	pail, **repair**, **soap**, **happy**
r	ride, **parent**, **wear**, **more**, **marry**
s	sit, **aside**, **pets**, **cent**, **pass**
sh	shoe, **washer**, **fish**, **mission**, **nation**
t	tag, **pretend**, **fat**, **button**, **dressed**
th	thin, **panther**, **both**
t͟h	this, **mother**, **smooth**
v	very, **favor**, **wave**
w	wet, **weather**, **reward**
y	yes, **onion**
z	zoo, **lazy**, **jazz**, **rose**, **dogs**, **houses**
zh	vision, **treasure**, **seizure**

DICTIONARY

A

a•bil•i•ty (ə bil´i tē) n. a•bil•i•ties The power to do something; skill. page-54

ach•ing (āk´ing) adj. Feeling pain. page-85

ac•ro•bat (ak´rə bat´) n. A person who can do difficult tricks, such as tumbling and balancing. page 36

ad•ven•ture (ad ven´chər) n. An exciting or unusual experience. page 54

ad•vice (ad vīs´) n. Helpful ideas. page 37

al•li•ga•tor (al´i gā´tər) n. A large crawling animal with a thick skin that lives in rivers and marshes. page 18

an•ces•tor (an´ses tər) n. Earlier member of one's family, such as a great grandfather. page 119

an•cient (ān´shənt) adj. Very old. page-30

ap•proach (ə prōch´) v. To come up to; come near. page 12

ar•e•a (âr´ē ə) n. Place. page 95

ar•range (ə rānj´) v. ar•ranged, ar•rang•ing To put something in a certain position or order. page 71

ath•lete (ath´lēt) n. Person trained in a sport or other activity that takes strength and skill. page 47

au•di•ence (ô´dē əns) n. The group of people who come to a place to see something. page 30

av•er•age (av´rij, av´ər ij) n. The usual number. page 95

B

bail (bāl) v. To throw water out of a boat with a bucket or pail. page 84

bal•anc•ing (bal´əns ing) adj. Keeping one's body in a steady position, usually one that is hard to hold. page 47

ba•ton (bə ton´) n. A short stick that a conductor uses to direct a musical group. page 109

beat (bēt) n. The pattern of loud and soft sounds in music. page 102

bee•tle (bē´təl) n. A kind of insect with hard, shiny front wings and thin back wings. page 108

be•gin•ning (bi gin´ing) n. The time when something began. page 54

be•neath (bi nēth´) prep. Under; below. page 95

birth (bûrth) n. Being born; starting life. page 90

bound (bound) v. To jump forward. page-13

brief•case (brēf´kās´) n. A case with a handle, used for carrying papers and books. page 109

bril•liant (bril´yənt) adj. Smart; clever. page 61

busi•ness (biz´nis) n. Something done to make money. page 37

C

calf (kaf) n. calves A baby cow, bull, or whale. page 90

cam•er•a (kam´ər ə, kam´rə) n. A machine that takes and sends pictures. page 114

camp•fire (kamp´fīr´) n. A fire used at a camp for cooking and warmth. page 54

can•vas (kan´vəs) n. A strong, heavy cloth used for tents and sails. page 37

ca•reer (kə rîr´) n. Job; the way a person makes a living. page 66

car•go (kär´gō) n. car•goes or car•gos Goods carried by a ship. page 78

car•toon (kär tün´) n. A movie made from drawings of made-up characters such as Donald Duck and Mickey Mouse. page-66

cause (kôz) v. caused, caus•ing To make something happen. page 102

cau•tion (kô´shən) n. Great care. page-42

cau•tious•ly (kô´shəs lē) adv. In a careful way. page 13

cel•e•brate (sel´ə brāt´) v. cel•e•brat•ed, cel•e•brat•ing To do something special for a certain day or event. page 119

cer•e•mo•ny (ser´ə mō´nē) n. cer•e•mo•nies A set of acts that are done for special events, such as a wedding or birth. page 119

chal•lenge (chal´ənj) n. Something that is hard to do. page 47

chant (chant) n. A short simple song sung over and over again. page 119

char•ac•ter (kar´ik tər) n. A person or animal in a book, play, or movie. page-66

choir (kwīr) n. A group of people who sing together. page 114

cli•mate (klī´mit) n. The kind of weather a place has. page 6

com•ic (kom´ik) adj. Funny. page 30

com•mand (kə mand´) n. An order to do something. page 42

com•mer•cial (kə mûr´shəl) n. A message that tries to get people to buy something; an ad. page 71

com•mu•ni•cate (kə mū´ni kāt´) v. com•mu•ni•cat•ed, com•mu•ni•cat•ing To send and receive messages. page 102

com•pan•ion (kəm pan´yən) n. Friend; one who keeps another company. page-42

com•pare (kəm pâr´) v. com•pared, com•par•ing To find out how two things are the same and how they are different. page 23

com•pos•er (kəm pō´zər) n. A person who makes up music. page 114

con•cert (kon´sərt) n. A musical show. page 114

con•di•tion (kən dish´ən) n. A person's health and strength. page 47

con•duc•tor (kən duk´tər) n. The person who directs a musical group. page 109

con•fi•dence (kon´fi dəns) n. Strong trust. page 47

con•ti•nent (kon´tə nənt) n. One of the seven large areas of land on the earth. page 18

cos•tume (kos´tüm, kos´tūm) n. Special clothing worn to look like someone or something else. page 30

count•less (kount´lis) adj. Too many to count. page 71

cre•at•ing (krē āt´ing) n. Making. page-71

crea•ture (krē´chər) n. An animal. page-90

crew (krü) n. A group of people who work together for a certain purpose, such as running a ship. page 78

cum•mer•bund (kum´ər bund´) n. A wide cloth belt usually worn with a tuxedo. page 108

cus•tom (kus´təm) n. Something usually done by a group of people. page 60

D

dance (dans) v. To move the feet and body in time to music. page 114

dan•ger•ous (dān´jər əs) adj. Not safe. page 42

daz•zling (daz´ling) adj. Amazing; exciting to watch. page 114

death (deth) n. The end of life. page 119

deck (dek) n. The floor of a ship. page 85

de•light (di līt´) v. To give pleasure. page-66

depths (depths) n. A deep place. page 95

de•vel•op (di vel´əp) v. To work out in detail. page 71

di•et (dī´it) n. The foods a person or animal usually eats. page 90

dif•fi•cult (dif´i kult´, dif´i kəlt) adj. Hard to do. page 47

di•no•saur (dī´nə sôr´) n. A type of animal that lived on the earth millions of years ago. page 6

dis•cov•er•y (dis kuv´ə rē) n. dis•cov•er•ies Something found for the first time. page 18

dis•tance (dis´təns) n. The space between two things. page 23

div•er (dī´vər) n. A person who works underwater. page 78

draw•ing (drô´ing) n. A picture made with a pen, pencil, crayon, or chalk. page 66

E

ef•fect (i fekt´) n. Something that happens because of something else; result. page-71

eld•er (el´dər) n. An older person. page-119

en•chant (en chant´) v. To please very much. page 66

en•cour•age•ment (en kûr´ij mənt, en kur´ij mənt) n. Something said or done to give hope and courage. page 85

en•er•gy (en´ər jē) n. en•er•gies The power to work and act. page 30

e•nor•mous (i nôr´məs) adj. Very large; huge. page 95

en•ter•tain (en´tər tān´) v. To keep people interested; to amuse. page 30

en•ter•tain•ment (en´tər tān´mənt) n. Something that pleases or interests people. page 66

e•vent (i vent´) n. A happening; something that takes place. page 30

ex•haust•ing (eg zôst´ing) adj. Making one very tired. page 47

ex•plor•er (ek splôr´ər) n. A person who travels to a place to discover new things. page 18

ex•tinct (ek stingkt´) adj. No longer found on the earth. page 6

F

fa•mous (fā´məs) adj. Known by many people. page 114

feast (fēst) n. A big meal made for a special event such as a holiday. page 60

fes•ti•val (fes´tə vəl) n. A special time for celebrating. page 119

fig•ure (fig´yər) n. Shape. page 71

fos•sil (fos´əl) n. The remains of a plant or animal of a past age. page 6

G

gasp (gasp) v. To take a quick, short breath. page 36

gloss•y (glô´sē) adj. gloss•i•er, gloss•i•est Shiny. page 37

grace•ful (grās´fəl) adj. Having a beautiful form; pleasing. page 47

grad•u•al•ly (graj´ü əl lē) adv. Happening slowly and steadily; bit by bit. page 42

grand•par•ent (grand´pâr´ənt) n. Grandfather or grandmother. page 119

gust (gust) n. A quick, strong rush of wind. page 84

H

hare (hâr) n. A kind of rabbit. page 12

har•vest (här´vist) n. The gathering of crops. page 119

height (hīt) n. The distance from top to bottom. page 23

hire (hīr) v. hired, hir•ing To pay money to use. page 37

hu•mor (hū´mər, ū´mər) n. What makes something funny. page 66

I

i•mage (im´ij) n. A likeness of a person, animal, or thing. page 71

i•mag•i•nar•y (i maj´ə ner´ē) adj. Not real; made-up. page 54

in•crease (in krēs´) v. in•creased, in•creas•ing To grow in size; add to. page 23

in•for•ma•tion (in´fər mā´shən) n. Facts; things that are known. page 6

in•stru•ment (in´strə mənt) n. Something that is played to make musical sounds. page 102

in•tel•li•gent (in tel´i jənt) adj. Smart; quick to learn. page 42

in•tent•ly (in tent´lē) adv. With close attention. page 30

J

jun•gle (jung´gəl) n. Hot, wet land with a thick growth of trees and bushes. page 6

K

knowl•edge (nol´ij) n. What is known; information. page 84

L

laugh•ter (laf´tər) n. Sounds people make when they are happy or amused. page 30

leg•end (lej´ənd) n. A made-up story about the past. page 54

leop•ard (lep´ərd) n. A big, fierce cat with a spotted coat. page 12

lev•el (lev´əl) n. Layer. page 23

liz•ard (liz´ərd) n. An animal with short legs, scaly skin, a long body, and a long tail. page 6

lumb•er (lum´bər) n. Wood that has been cut into boards. page 18

M

mak•er (mā´kər) n. A person who makes or builds. page 37

mam•mal (mam´əl) n. Warm-blooded animals that have a backbone, such as horses, humans, and whales. page 90

mam•moth (mam´əth) adj. Very large; huge. page 95

mas•sive (mas´iv) adj. Heavy; large. page-90

mast (mast) n. A long pole that holds a ship's sails. page 78

mas•ter (mas´tər) adj. Expert. page 84

ma•te•ri•al (mə tîr´ē əl) n. Something goods can be made of. page 18

mel•o•dy (mel´ə dē) n. mel•o•dies Tune. page 114

me•ter (mē´tər) n. A measure of length, just over 39 inches. page 23

min•er•al (min´ər əl) n. A material like gold or coal that is dug out of the earth. page 18

mir•ror (mir´ər) n. A glass that sends back light and shows a picture of things in front of it. page 108

moist (moist) adj. A little wet; damp. page-6

mos•qui•to (mə skē´tō) n. mo•squi•toes or mo•squi•tos A small flying insect that bites people. page 18

mo•tion (mō´shən) n. Movement. page-71

mus•cle (mus´əl) n. The parts of the body used to move other parts. page 47

mu•si•cal (mū´zi kəl) adj. Able to make music. page 102

N

nu•mer•ous (nü´mər əs, nū´mər əs) adj. Many; great in number. page 23

O

or•chard (ôr´chərd) n. A piece of land on which many fruit trees are grown. page-54

or•ches•tra (ôr´ke strə) n. A large group of musicians who play music together. page 109

out•grow (out´grō´) v. To lose in growing up; to leave behind. page 37

P

part•ner (pärt´nər) n. A person who joins with others in a business. page 37

ped•al (ped´əl) n. A part of a machine that is moved by the foot. page 102

per•form•er (pər fôr´mər) n. A person who entertains the public. page 47

pi•lot (pī´lət) n. A person who flies an airplane. page 18

pi•rate (pī´rit) n. A person who robs ships at sea. page 78

pitch (pich) n. The lowness or highness of a sound. page 102

pleas•ant (plez´ənt) adj. Pleasing; enjoyable. page 12

plen•ty (plen´tē) n. All that is needed. page 95

pre•serve (pri zûrv´) v. pre•served, pre•serv•ing To keep safe; keep the same for a long time. page 6

pro•fes•sion•al (prə fesh´ə nəl) adj. Getting paid to do something that others do for fun; expert. page 30

pro•tec•tion (prə tek´shən) n. Something that keeps one from danger or harm. page 42

R

rag•ing (rāj´ing) adj. Filled with high waves; wild. page 85

re•fuse (ri fūz´) v. re•fused, re•fus•ing To turn down; say no. page 60

re•spond (ri spond´) v. To act in answer to something said or done. page 42

rub•ber (rub´ər) n. Milky juice of certain plants used to make things like tires and balls. page 18

S

sail•boat (sāl´bōt´) n. A boat that uses sails to move. page 78

sail•or (sā´lər) n. A person who works on a ship. page 78

scarce (skârs) adj. scarc•er, scarc•est Hard to find; small in amount. page 95

scoop (sküp) v. To hollow out by digging. page 54

sim•ply (sim´plē) adv. Just; only. page 60

sing•er (sing´ər) n. A person who sings. page 114

skull (skul) n. The bones of the head. page-6

snarl (snärl) v. To growl in an angry way. page 13

spar•kle (spär´kəl) v. spar•kled, spar•kling To shine; give off flashes of light. page-60

squall (skwôl) n. A sudden, strong windstorm. page 84

squeeze (skwēz) v. squeezed, squeez•ing To press together. page 61

stool (stül) n. A chair that has no back. page 109

struck (struk) v. past tense of strike; struck or strick•en; strik•ing Hit. page-102

stu•di•o (stü´dē ō´, stū´dē ō´) n. A place where movies are made. page 66

suc•cess•ful (sək ses´fəl) adj. Having reached a goal such as gaining fame or respect. page 114

sup•ply (sə plī´) v. sup•plied, sup•ply•ing To give something needed. page 23

sur•face (sûr´fis) n. The top of something. page 95

swell (swel) n. A tall ocean wave. page 84

sym•pho•ny (sim´fə nē) n. sym•pho•nies A long piece of music, usually made up of four different parts called movements. page 109

T

tale (tāl) n. A story. page 54

tal•ent (tal´ənt) n. Natural skill in art, sports, or some other area. page 66

tame (tām) v. tamed, tam•ing To train a wild animal to be gentle and to obey. page 42

tel•e•vi•sion (tel´ə vizh´ən) n. A machine that receives signals and shows pictures with sound. page 71

ter•ri•fy•ing (ter´ə fī´ing) adj. Frightening; scary. page 12

thick (thik) adj. Crowded; set close together. page 23

thou•sand (thou´zənd) n. Ten hundred; 1,000. page 23

thrash•ing (thrash´ing) n. A beating. page-13

tight•en (tī´tən) v. To make tighter; stretch. page 102

ton (tun) n. 2,240 pounds. page 90

trade (trād) adj. Having to do with buying and selling goods. page 78

train•er (trā´nər) n. A person who teaches tricks to animals. page 42

treas•ure (trezh´ər) n. Something worth a lot of money. page 78

trem•ble (trem´bəl) v. trem•bled, trem•bling To shake. page 12

tribe (trīb) n. A group of people who live together as a community. page 119

tux•e•do (tuk sē´dō) n. A suit with shiny material on the collar and pants, usually worn for special events. page-108

U

un•der•wa•ter (un´dər wô´tər, un´dər wot´ər) adv. Below the surface of the water. page 90

un•u•su•al•ly (un ū´zhü əl lē) adv. In a way that is not usual or common. page-60

V

vast (vast) adj. Very large. page 95

vol•ume (vol´ūm) n. The amount of sound. page 102

waist (wāst) n. The part of the body between the chest and the hips. page 61

weigh (wā) v. To be as heavy as. page 90

whale (hwāl, wāl) n. A huge mammal that lives in the sea. page 90

wil•der•ness (wil´dər nis) n. wil•der•ness•es A wild place where no people live. page 54

wreck (rek) n. What is left of something that was broken or destroyed. page 78

yam (yam) n. A sweet potato. page 60

ANSWER KEY

UNIT 1
Jungles and Tropics

LESSON 1
The Age of the Dinosaur

Context Clues

1. dinosaurs 6. lizard
2. information 7. moist
3. preserved 8. jungle
4. fossils 9. climate
5. skull 10. extinct

Antonyms

1. preserved 3. extinct
2. moist 4. jungle

Dictionary Skills

1. skull 4. climate
2. lizard 5. dinosaur
3. fossils

Hidden Message Puzzle

1. information 5. jungle
2. dinosaur 6. moist
3. climate 7. preserved
4. skull 8. extinct

Answer to puzzle: footprints

Get Wise to Tests

1. B 3. A 5. C 7. D 9. D
2. H 4. G 6. H 8. F 10. H

Writing

Answers will vary based on students' personal experiences.

LESSON 2
Rhinos for Lunch and Elephants for Supper!

Using Context

1. cautiously 6. bounded
2. hare 7. thrashing
3. trembled 8. pleasant
4. snarled 9. approached
5. terrifying 10. leopard

Challenge Yourself

Possible responses: tiger, bear

Dictionary Skills

approached, bounded, cautiously, hare; leopard, pleasant, terrifying, thrashing

Synonyms

cautiously, pleasant, trembled, snarled

Get Wise to Tests

1. D 3. A 5. B 7. D 9. D
2. H 4. H 6. G 8. H 10. G

Writing

Answers will vary based on students' personal experiences.

LESSON 3
Amazon Riches

Using Context

1. lumber 6. rubber
2. explorers 7. mosquitoes
3. materials 8. discoveries
4. continent 9. pilot
5. minerals 10. alligators

Classifying

Products: lumber, minerals
Animals: mosquitoes, alligators
People: explorers

Cloze Paragraph

1. continent 4. material
2. discoveries 5. minerals
3. pilot

Get Wise to Tests

1. A 3. B 5. B 7. C 9. B
2. G 4. I 6. G 8. G 10. I

Writing

Answers will vary based on students' personal experiences.

LESSON 4
A World Below the Trees

Using Context

1. numerous 6. supply
2. height 7. distance
3. increase 8. compare
4. meter 9. thick
5. thousand 10. levels

Challenge Yourself

Possible responses: my height, my classroom

Synonyms

1. increases 3. supply
2. numerous 4. levels

Writing Sentences

Answers will vary based on students' personal experiences.

Word Game

1. meter 6. increase
2. compare 7. distance
3. numerous 8. thick
4. supply 9. height
5. thousand 10. levels

Answer to puzzle: many snakes

Get Wise to Tests

1. a measure 6. many
2. make greater 7. how tall
3. crowded together 8. space
4. give 9. see how alike
5. stages 10. large number

Review

1. flying insects 2. searchers

Writing

Answers will vary based on students' personal experiences.

UNIT 2
In the Spotlight

LESSON 5
Tell Me a Story

Using Context

1. entertain 6. comic
2. ancient 7. costume
3. energy 8. professional
4. audience 9. intently
5. event 10. laughter

Challenge Yourself

Possible responses: Mickey Mouse, Bugs Bunny

Multiple Meanings

1. b 2. a 3. a 4. b

Cloze Paragraph

1. event 4. audience
2. costume 5. laughter
3. entertain

Crossword Puzzle

Across
1. professional
4. energy
5. ancient
7. intently
9. entertain

Down
2. event
3. laughter
5. audience
6. costume
8. comic

Get Wise to Tests

1. professional 6. comic
2. costume 7. audience
3. event 8. laughter
4. intently 9. entertain
5. ancient 10. energy

Writing

Answers will vary based on students' personal experiences.

LESSON 6
The Ringling Brothers

Context Clues

1. business 6. hired
2. partner 7. acrobat
3. canvas 8. gasped
4. glossy 9. outgrow
5. advice 10. makers

Challenge Yourself

Possible responses: play ball, play checkers

Dictionary Skills

1. advice 4. glossy
2. hired 5. canvas
3. business

Writing Sentences

Answers will vary based on students' personal experiences.

Get Wise to Tests

1. C 3. D 5. D 7. B 9. A
2. F 4. F 6. H 8. H 10. I

Writing

Answers will vary based on students' personal experiences.

LESSON 7
Lights, Camera, Action!

Using Context

1. respond
2. trainers
3. caution
4. protection
5. gradually
6. dangerous
7. companions
8. tame
9. commands
10. intelligent

Challenge Yourself

Possible responses: sit, stay

Cloze Paragraph

1. tame
2. trainers
3. respond
4. gradually
5. commands
6. companions

Antonyms

1. dangerous
2. intelligent
3. caution
4. gradually
5. protection

Get Wise to Tests

1. make gentle
2. teachers
3. bit by bit
4. not safe
5. smart
6. orders
7. answer
8. friends
9. safety
10. care

Review

1. expert
2. listeners
3. happening
4. funny

Writing

Answers will vary based on students' personal experiences.

LESSON 8
The Spinning Star

Context Clues

1. athlete
2. difficult, balancing
3. condition
4. muscles
5. graceful
6. confidence
7. challenge
8. performer
9. exhausting

Synonyms

1. exhausting
2. confidence
3. difficult
4. athlete

Dictionary Skills

1. graceful: having a beautiful form; pleasing
2. challenge: something that is hard to do
3. performer: a person who entertains the public
4. balancing: keeping one's body in a steady position, usually one that is hard to hold
5. condition: a person's health and strength
6. muscles: the parts of the body used to move other parts
7. confidence: strong trust
8. exhausting: making one very tired
9. athlete: person trained in a sport or other activity that takes strength and skill

Word Map

What she is: a performer, an athlete
What she has: body muscles, confidence in herself
What she faces: big challenges, exhausting work
What kind of tricks she does: difficult/balancing tricks, balancing/difficult acts
What she has to be: very graceful, in good condition

Get Wise to Tests

1. C 3. B 5. C 7. B 9. C
2. G 4. F 6. G 8. F 10. H

Review

1. B 2. F

Writing

Answers will vary based on students' personal experiences.

UNIT 3
Imaginary Characters

LESSON 9
Mighty Paul Bunyan

Context clues

1. campfire
2. tale
3. imaginary, wilderness
4. ability, orchard
5. legends
6. adventures, scoops
7. beginnings

Challenge Yourself

Possible responses: Nate the Great, Ramona

Dictionary Skills

1. both are stories
2. ability
3. adventures
4. trees
5. Possible answers: sit around it to keep warm; cook over it

Writing Sentences

Answers will vary based on students' personal experiences.

Tangled-Up Words

1. imaginary
2. campfires
3. tale
4. orchard
5. scoops
6. legends
7. adventures
8. wilderness
9. beginnings
10. ability

Get Wise to Tests

1. A 3. A 5. B 7. C 9. D
2. H 4. I 6. G 8. F 10. G

Review

1. C 2. I

Writing

Answers will vary based on students' personal experiences.

LESSON 10
How Spider Got a Thin Waist

Context Clues

1. yams
2. sparkled
3. feast
4. simply
5. refuse
6. custom
7. unusually
8. brilliant
9. waist
10. squeezed

Antonyms

1. refuse
2. brilliant
3. unusually

Cloze Paragraph

1. custom
2. feast
3. Yams
4. sparkled
5. waist
6. simply
7. squeezed

Get Wise to Tests

1. B 3. B 5. C 7. B 9. D
2. H 4. F 6. I 8. F 10. F

Writing

Answers will vary based on students' personal experiences.

LESSON 11
The Mickey Mouse Man

Using Context

1. career
2. studio
3. drawings
4. delighted
5. entertainment
6. cartoons
7. enchanted
8. characters
9. humor
10. talent

Classifying

What He Created Himself: drawings, characters, cartoons
How He Made People Feel: delighted, enchanted

Writing Sentences

Answers will vary based on students' personal experiences.

Get Wise to Tests

1. D 3. C 5. C 7. D 9. B
2. F 4. I 6. G 8. F 10. G

Review

1. A 2. H

Writing

Answers will vary based on students' personal experiences.

LESSON 12
Computer Cartoons

Using Context

1. images
2. develop
3. television
4. motion
5. commercial
6. countless
7. arrange
8. figure
9. creating
10. effect

Cloze Paragraph

1. television
2. commercial
3. countless
4. creating

Multiple Meanings

1. b 2. a 3. a 4. b

Dictionary Skills

commercial, countless, creating
develop, effect, figure

Classifying

What Artists Do: develop, arrange
What Artists Can Make: commercial, images, figure

Get Wise to Tests

1. D 3. C 5. C 7. C 9. A
2. I 4. I 6. G 8. I 10. F

Review

1. C 2. F

Writing

Answers will vary based on students' personal experiences.

UNIT 4
Water Everywhere

LESSON 13
Tressure Under the Sea

Using Context

1. treasures	6. crew
2. cargo	7. trade
3. sailors	8. masts
4. wreck	9. pirate
5. sailboats	10. divers

Synonyms

1. poles, masts	3. cargo, goods
2. treasures, riches	4. robber, pirate

Classifying

1. sailboat	4. crew
2. Treasures	5. Wrecks
3. Cargo	

Word Map

People on a Ship: pirates, crew, sailors, divers
Parts of a Ship: mast
Things Carried on a Ship: cargo, treasures
Kinds of Ships: sailboat, trade
Additional answers will vary.

Get Wise to Tests

1. B 3. A 5. A 7. B 9. C
2. I 4. H 6. I 8. G 10. H

Writing

Answers will vary based on students' personal experiences.

LESSON 14
Storm at Sea

Context Clues

1. knowledge	6. bailed
2. master	7. gust
3. squall	8. aching
4. raging	9. encouragement
5. swells	10. deck

Multiple Meanings

1. a 2. b 3. b 4. a

Dictionary Skills

1. knowledge: what is known; information
2. squall: a sudden, strong windstorm
3. raging: filled with high waves; wild
4. bailed: threw water out of a boat with a bucket or pail
5. gust: a quick, strong rush of wind
6. encouragement: something said or done to give hope and courage
7. aching: feeling pain
8. master: expert

Get Wise to Tests

1. C 3. B 5. A 7. B 9. D
2. F 4. H 6. I 8. F 10. H

Writing

Answers will vary based on students' personal experiences.

LESSON 15
A Whale of a Story

Context Clues

1. whale	6. massive
2. calf	7. creature
3. birth	8. diet
4. weigh	9. underwater
5. tons	10. mammals

Word Groups

1. massive	3. diet
2. mammals	4. tons

Dictionary Skills

birth, calf, creature, diet; tons, underwater, weigh, whale

Get Wise to Tests

1. whale	6. underwater
2. weigh	7. diet
3. creature	8. mammals
4. birth	9. massive
5. tons	10. calf

Writing

Answers will vary based on students' personal experiences.

LESSON 16
Life in the Sea

Using Context

1. depths	6. scarce
2. average	7. beneath
3. enormous	8. plenty
4. mammoth	9. surface
5. areas	10. vast

Challenge yourself

Possible responses: elephant, rhinoceros

Synonyms

1. mammoth	4. areas
2. depth	5. average
3. beneath	

Antonyms

1. scarce	4. surface
2. plenty	5. beneath
3. enormous	

Word Game

1. scarce	6. mammoth
2. vast	7. areas
3. average	8. enormous
4. depths	9. plenty
5. surface	10. beneath

Answer to puzzle: cave

Get Wise to Tests

1. huge	6. deepest part
2. below	7. enough
3. places	8. usual
4. rare	9. very big
5. very great	10. top

Review

1. baby 2. food

Writing

Answers will vary based on students' personal experiences.

UNIT 5
Making Music

LESSON 17
There Is Music in the Air

Using Context

1. musical	6. pitch
2. communicate	7. tighten
3. cause	8. volume
4. pedals	9. beat
5. instrument	10. struck

Word Groups

1. volume	3. cause
2. struck	4. communicate

Cloze Paragraph

1. instrument	4. pitch
2. tighten	5. beat
3. pedals	6. musical

Word Map

Some parts: pedals
How played: struck
Sound: pitch, volume
Care: tighten
Reason played: communicate ideas, musical entertainment

Get Wise to Tests

1. C 3. A 5. C 7. C 9. A
2. G 4. H 6. G 8. G 10. H

Writing

Answers will vary based on students' personal experiences.

LESSON 18
The Philharmonic Gets Dressed

Context clues

1. orchestra
2. tuxedo
3. cummerbund
4. mirrors
5. beetle
6. briefcase
7. stools
8. conductor
9. baton
10. symphony

Word Sense

Possible answers:

1. school briefcase
2. man's cummerbund
3. yes
4. black beetle
5. yes
6. tuxedo jacket
7. orchestra plays

Music Words

1. orchestra
2. baton
3. conductor
4. symphony

Get Wise to Tests

1. C 2. I 3. A 4. G 5. D 6. H 7. A 8. F 9. B 10. F

Writing

Answers will vary based on students' personal experiences.

LESSON 19
The Boys Choir of Harlem

Using Context

1. dance
2. singer
3. choir
4. melodies
5. composers
6. camera
7. concerts
8. dazzling
9. successful
10. famous

Word Groups

1. melodies
2. famous
3. dazzling
4. composers
5. dance

Cloze Paragraph

1. singer
2. melodies
3. concerts
4. dance
5. successful

Get Wise to Tests

1. B 2. F 3. C 4. F 5. C 6. H 7. D 8. I 9. B 10. I

Writing

Answers will vary based on students' personal experiences.

LESSON 20
Special Times for Music

Using Context

1. festival
2. ceremony
3. chants
4. harvest
5. celebrate
6. elders
7. tribe
8. death
9. ancestors
10. grandparents

Word Groups

1. grandparent
2. festival
3. celebrate
4. death

Dictionary Skills

Possible answers:

1. It is a family member who lived long ago.
2. yes
3. They are songs with special pat terns.
4. yes

Hidden Message Puzzle

1. chant
2. ancestor
3. death
4. festival
5. elders
6. ceremony
7. tribe
8. celebrate

Answer to puzzle: holidays

Get Wise to Tests

1. C 2. G 3. A 4. H 5. D 6. I 7. B 8. F 9. B 10. H

Review

1. A 2. G

Writing

Answers will vary based on students' personal experiences.

UNIT 1 Review

1. increase
2. height
3. extinct
4. lumber
5. continent
6. approached
7. terrifying
8. moist

UNIT 2 Review

1. yes
2. no
3. no
4. yes
5. yes
6. no
7. yes
8. no
9. yes
10. no

UNIT 3 Review

1. enchanted
2. talent
3. orchard
4. television
5. arrange
6. refuse
7. sparkled
8. imaginary

UNIT 4 Review

1. no
2. no
3. yes
4. yes
5. no
6. yes
7. no
8. no
9. no
10. yes

UNIT 5 Review

1. famous
2. baton
3. celebrate
4. struck
5. tuxedo
6. communicate
7. dazzling
8. ancestors

REVIEW AND WRITE

Answers will vary based on students' personal experiences.